D1026695

When Steepl

WHEN STEEPLES CRY

leading congregations
through loss and change

JACO J. HAMMAN

The Pilgrim Press
Cleveland

To Michelle:

For living a loss with me

The Pilgrim Press

700 Prospect Avenue

Cleveland, Ohio 44115-1100

Pilgrimpress.com

© 2005 by Jaco J. Hamman

Printed in the United States of America on acid-free paper

09 08 07 06 05 5 4 3 2 1

Library of Congress Cataloging-in-Publication Data

Hamman, Jaco J.

    When steeples cry : leading congregations through loss and change /

    Jaco J. Hamman.

      p. cm.

    ISBN 0-8298-1694-1 (alk. paper)

    1. Loss (Psychology)—Religious aspects—Christianity. 2. Bereavement—Religious aspects—Christianity. 3. Grief—Religious aspects—Christianity. 4. Change (Psychology)—Religious aspects—Christianity. 5. Life change events—Religious aspects—Christianity. 6. Pastoral theology. I. Title.

BV4905.3.H37 2005

253'.7—dc22   2005023958

+ Contents +

+ Acknowledgments +

I AM INDEBTED TO SEVERAL HUNDRED people and numerous congregations, each one enriching my reflection during speaking engagements, consultations with congregations, conferences, workshops, breakfasts, or meetings over a cup of coffee or tea.

I am grateful to Jon Berquist, who first believed in the importance of this project and its timeliness for the Church of Christ.

I especially want to thank the first readers of the manuscript, Sharon Arendshorst, Justin Meyers, Rick Patterson, Chad Pierce, The Pot-Stirrers (Stan Rock, Earl Laman, Les Beach, Jean Scholten, Mike Henry, and Darrell Schregardus), and the students enrolled in the elective I teach, Ministry as Grief Work.

Beth Smith not only read the first draft of every chapter, but she helped me clear my calendar when I needed time to work on the manuscript.

I am grateful to Tom Boogaart, George Brown, Steven Chase, Leanne Van Dyk, and my other colleagues at Western Theological Seminary for their constant support and encouragement.

My parents in Port Elizabeth (South Africa), Barry and Maria, never left my mind during this project. *Pa, Ma, my lewe hier is julle verlies.*

My wife and best friend, Michelle, for living with me as I worked in the early morning hours and became too tired to be present late at night. And Jami and Michaela, *my engele,* for enriching my life beyond my imagination.

I want to express my appreciation to Ulrike Guthrie, editor at The Pilgrim Press. Uli, your guidance formed this project into the personal autobiography it is. Our conversations urged me to write from my soul.

Finally, I am grateful that I am in a covenant with the God who mourns and who is the Fountain of life.

+ Introduction +

The Spirit of the Lord God is upon me,
Because the Lord has anointed me
God has sent me as a herald of joy to the humble,
To bind up the wounded of heart.

(Isa. 61:1–2)[1]

A S A LEADER IN YOUR CONGREGATION you facilitate growth and bring change. You are called to empower your congregation to be the body of Christ. Inevitably, your call includes not only being with those who grieve and mourn, but introducing loss to your congregation. The face of change-as-loss is varied and always morphing into a new image: a congregation is thriving with rapid membership growth; a pastor leaves; a congregation commits to a building project; a church member dies; programs are introduced and then disappear; a congregation becomes an island in a sea of societal change. Your effectiveness and creativeness as an agent of growth and vitality for your congregation depends on your ability to facilitate the work of mourning.

The prophet Isaiah describes his call as restoring justice to an unjust world and leading a grieving people beyond despair. For us in congregational leadership, our call narrative is a shelter against storms, an aquifer with nourishing water when ministry becomes a desert. Isaiah's call narrative forms a core biblical foundation and is woven into this book. Isaiah states:

The Spirit of the Sovereign Lord is on me, because the Lord has anointed me to preach good news to the poor. He has sent me to bind up the brokenhearted, to proclaim freedom for the captives and release from darkness for the prisoners, to proclaim the year of the Lord's favor and the day of vengeance of our God, to comfort all who mourn, and provide for those who grieve in Zion—to bestow on them a crown of beauty instead of ashes, the oil of gladness instead of mourning, and a garment of praise instead of a spirit of despair. (Isa. 61:1–4)[2]

The two themes introduced here by Isaiah—bringing good news to the disenfranchised and the promise of restoration imbedded in doing the work of mourning—are guideposts for today's church leaders. As a leader in your congregation, you are called, as Isaiah was, to bring good news to all people, to seek justice for all, and to comfort those who mourn. At first glance we might think we can "preach" our congregations into changing the way they live as the body of Christ or to move beyond despair. But the translation of the verb "to preach" is a rather poor one. The Hebrew word used is *basher,* from the stem *bashar,* which literally means meat or flesh. Isaiah 61:1 states: "The Spirit of the Sovereign Lord is on [you], because the Lord has anointed [you] to ENFLESH or EMBODY good news to the poor. . . ."

Preaching elicits visions of speaking. Embodiment is about being. Preaching implies preparation and an hour of performance. Embodiment is 24/7/365; a way of being with people and a way of seeing the world. *What is your call narrative?* Is facilitating the work of mourning—leading people from grief and despair to gladness—a central task you have identified for yourself? And in what ways do you enflesh your ministry?

When Steeples Cry is about embodiment, yours and mine. It is not meant to be a "how-to" book, but it envisions you being a different kind of leader to your community. Written primarily, but not exclusively, for church leaders and those seminarians who will serve in mainline Protestant denominations, *When Steeples Cry* identifies the work of mourning as a significant aspect of being a church leader in North America today. Leading your congregation towards gratitude, gladness, and praise, to rebuild ruins and to be a tree of righteousness (Isa. 61:3b–4) is a difficult call, especially if one accepts recent statistics about declining membership in Protestant denominations.

STATISTICS

Mainline Protestant denominations have been losing members at a rate of between a half and one (0.5–1.0) percent per year. Some denominations have maintained that rate of decline for more than forty years! Many millions of people are represented in the following statistics spanning a forty-year period:[3]

- The United Methodist Church (USA) has lost more than 3.3 million members.
- The Presbyterian Church (USA) has lost more than 2.3 million members since 1971. These numbers include a denominational split that year.
- The Episcopal Church (USA) has lost more than 1.1 million members.
- The Evangelical Lutheran Church (in America) has lost more than 540,000 members, including a loss of 61,871 members from 2001–2. Forty-five congregations closed their doors in 2002.
- The Reformed Church in America (RCA) has lost more than 50,000 members since it peaked at 225,000 members in the 1960s.
- The Christian Reformed Church in North America (CRCNA; 278,944 members) has lost more than 42,000 members during the period 1992–2002.
- Despite the fact that 80 new congregations joined the United Church of Christ (UCC) during the past two years, 32 percent of the denomination's congregations are losing members; 52 percent are staying the same, and only 16 percent of congregations are growing. In 1999, UCC membership declined by 19,406 members (1.37 percent). A total of 36 congregations closed their doors and 41 congregations withdrew from the denomination.

How does your denomination's situation impact your congregation? What do the membership trends of your congregation tell you?

Of course there are many reasons for the membership loss identified here. Aging denominations have many deaths. The birth rate amongst White Anglo-Saxon Protestant (WASP) people has declined greatly, and rural America is experiencing significant depopulation. Social and religious values have shifted, and a consumerist culture has grown. The demographics of most towns and cities have changed greatly due to economic reasons and immigration patterns. Members left established congregations as denominational loyalty declined. Furthermore, loss is constantly created and intensified as congregations make radical changes to their worship styles or to their administrative structures to adapt to an ever-changing society.

Knowing why the losses occurred or trying to understand postmodern culture does not necessarily facilitate the work of mourning in a congregation and does not prevent future losses from occurring. A search for such knowledge can be a defense against the painful awareness that the body of Christ is vulnerable to loss. The numbers might even be deceptive, since they do not indicate the magnitude and multidimensional nature of the loss that denominations and many congregations experienced and are still experiencing. Rather, the qualitative nature of loss is multifaceted, calling for wide-ranging identification of loss and grief and intentional mourning by the body of Christ. Whether you want to admit it or not, loss and grief describe the story of your congregation, even if your community is part of the 51 percent of all congregations in North America that are growing![4] Rather than attempting to explain the losses in your congregation, *When Steeples Cry* empowers you to identify the losses that are influencing your congregation and guides you on how to facilitate the work of mourning.

GRIEF AND (THE WORK OF) MOURNING

Two words that are featured prominently throughout this book are grief and mourning. You will be empowered to recognize grief reactions and to facilitate "the work of mourning" in your congregation. *Grief is the normal emotional, spiritual, physical, and relational reaction to the experience of loss and change.* It is a powerful and involuntary force governing the way your congregation will have its life together and engage God and the world. Your congregation will experience a vocal or silent grief reaction with every change you intentionally initiate or that occurs "naturally" in the life of the church. Grief within a person or a congregation, like wind, water, and fire, takes enormous amounts of energy to control. Grief can be mute, without any voice. In caregiving and through a pastoral presence, however, mourning brings to voice the unmentionables of your congregation's life.

Mourning, in contrast, is the intentional process of letting go of relationships, dreams, and visions as your congregation lives into a new identity after the experience of loss and change. Mourning implies living through grief; to live with loss and change. Due to its intentionality, mourning is work. Mourning requires mindfulness and decries nostalgia. You have to embrace Paul's challenge to the believers in Rome, whom he commanded to have "sober judgment" about being the body of Christ (Rom. 12:3).

Doing the work of mourning is not about replacement but describes a process of evoking memories of the past, discerning the impact of change on the present, envisioning a future, and then living into that new identity. The work of mourning is a creative response to loss. If you see yourself as a church leader who is called to lead your congregation toward renewal and revitalization or to be faithful and fruitful, facilitating the work of mourning will be a central task.

YOUR CONGREGATION AS A GOSPEL COMMUNITY

The Australian theologian and anthropologist Gerald Arbuckle systematically addresses the dynamics of loss and grief within congregations. He wrote two books on the topic, but it is especially the second book, *Change, grief and renewal in the church: A spirituality for a new era* (1991), which has taught me.[5] In his books, Arbuckle describes congregations in terms of "apostolic groups," "Gospel communities," or even "pilgrim communities." In today's culture, "church" often refers to a building and not to a group of individuals called to carry the Gospel of Jesus Christ to the world.

I find the description of a congregation as a Gospel community challenging yet inviting. It challenges every congregation to have a missional nature, to be good news to the poor. But it also invites visions of community, of a group of people being brought together in

Christ and by God. There is richness within the term "Gospel community" that is sorely lacking in the term "church." Whereas church has a very specific connotation, a Gospel community can be a congregation, a cell group or a basic Christian community, a leadership team or a larger group such as a denomination, a hospital, a school, or another institution, even a family. As you will discover, I shy away from "church-language." I prefer the term *Gospel community* to refer to a congregation or any other communities of believers gathering to be together in God's service. My ministry setting is a theological seminary, and even if we are not a "church," we certainly are a Gospel community.

Every Gospel community in *When Steeples Cry* is a community "created" for the purpose of writing the book. I have drawn on fifteen years of being a pastoral leader with various roles in different communities to envision the diverse ways leaders experience their ministry and the ways change and loss influence the body of Christ. I envision you recognizing yourself in the pastors and congregations you will meet in the pages to come.

WHEN STEEPLES CRY AS AUTOBIOGRAPHY

Just as you have been prepared to lead your Gospel community, so life has taught me about the ever-presence of loss and the importance of embracing the work of mourning. Born into a white, Dutch Reformed family who lived just outside Johannesburg, South Africa, I experienced going to school at the age of six as a significant loss. I never went to any preschool activities, and although I looked forward to attending school, I experienced "losing" my mother as traumatic. I could not mourn and in my grief relied on food to bring comfort to my soul. For the next thirty years I would be overweight. Numerous times as I worked on chapters of this book, an unwelcome hunger came over me.

At the age of ten we moved to a coastal town. I took my low self-esteem and poor body image with me. The loss of home and friends, and especially our beloved basset hound, Flappie, the puppy that became a dog with a deep but friendly bark, impacted my body greatly. I developed severe asthma within weeks. As family and doctors rationalized reasons for the sudden onset of childhood asthma, never was an emotional cause identified as a possible origin. The unspoken grief entered my body. It took more than twenty years for me to do the work of mourning, and now I no longer have (or need) asthma. I had to be an adult to work through the grief and sadness of the ten-year-old boy who lost the air that he breathed.

Since 1993 I have been an immigrant. Immigrants live a life of loss, irrespective of what is gained by moving to one's adopted country. Seeing my family as I enter the arrivals room of an airport awakens in me the six-year-old boy who desperately wanted to stay home. Leaving them behind an inch-thick glass wall in the departure hall instantaneously reminds me of the ten year old leaving home and friends and a beloved pet behind. Both experiences typically unleash unbearable sobs. I cry freely, my body aching. I envision God writing my tears on a scroll or catching them in a bottle (Ps. 56:8). For immigrants, even ones like me carrying two passports and building a family in my adopted country, the relinquishment of everything mother-like (mothers, fathers, siblings, a mother tongue, land/earth, familiar foods, tastes and smells, and more), reoccurs with every anniversary or milestone in life.

Various communities have taught me about the impact and corrosive power of loss on a group of people. The denomination that gave me my faith, the Dutch Reformed Church in South Africa (DRCSA), lost apartheid. The DRCSA was the primary supporter of the white nationalist apartheid government. When democracy came to South Africa in 1994, the DRCSA awakened to a changed world. Apartheid was experienced as "good" to the DRCSA. Despite engaging in this self-confessed sinful behavior, the denomination received power, prestige, and protection, a privileged position. More than a decade after the fall of apartheid and the arrival of democracy, the DRCSA is still searching for an identity that can help them be a Gospel community in Africa. They remain primarily an irrelevant white denomination in a black society besieged by crime, HIV/AIDS, and poverty. *But how do you grieve something that you have confessed as a sin?* This paradox cannot be solved, for the body of Christ does not live only theologically, ecumenically, or even ethically, but also emotionally and relationally. The DRCSA as a denomination and most of their congregations remain stuck due to the dynamics of grief.

A second community that taught me about communal grief was a therapeutic community in New York City. I was enrolled in a three-year pastoral psychotherapy and marriage and family program when, in my second year, there were significant changes in the administration. Out of protest, a large number of the faculty resigned, leaving us with persons we perceived as responsible for the pain that entered our community. Oddly enough, this therapeutic community could not engage in the kind of conversation that could facilitate healing. The community mirrored the break-up between Sigmund Freud and Carl Gustav Jung, the theoretical fathers of the administrators involved. It is now some years after the change in administration took place, and the institute is still searching for a redefined identity.

A third community that is currently teaching me about the impact of change on a group of people is the seminary where I teach. The seminary is growing faster than we can manage. Even as we are blessed with higher enrollment numbers, we see changes all around us: more students; additional faculty and staff; changes in administration; a new building; two new academic programs; search committees; and more. We are growing so fast that we may not know who we are at this moment. Are we a small seminary with a family feel, or are we a midsize seminary where more formalized administrative processes and sufficient support staff need to be in place? How is all the change around us impacting the workload for faculty and staff? Can we keep doing things in the same way if we have more than doubled in size in less than ten years?

These are important questions. I hear tension amongst the faculty and staff. Students are frustrated that faculty cannot give them the time they demand. We do not have support services in place for a community this size. Although we can name the changes I identified, and others might say that we are a midsize seminary, it seems as if having a conversation about how our identity is changing and how we are living into this loss is far more difficult.

My vocation is that of being a teacher of pastoral care for the next generation of pastors in the church of Christ. I have learned that living into this call requires continually doing the work of mourning. A year ago I arranged an education event for the students at my school as called for by my job description. I convened a student forum and asked the students how I could be of service to them. A group of about ten students indicated they want to learn more about how to maintain appropriate boundaries in ministry. I sought a pastoral counselor in town who would be willing to lead a three-hour workshop on the topic "Keeping Covenant: Understanding and Honoring Your Personal and Professional Boundaries." Everything was arranged a few months in advance for a Saturday morning workshop. A few days before the workshop I cancelled the event because only two students had signed up. I was angry and felt betrayed, telling myself that I will not arrange events for the Student Assistance Program, a program I initiated, the following semester. But I mourned the disappointment, and this year I will risk organizing new workshops.

Conversation about a difficult topic, such as loss, has always been hard for Gospel communities, even the one of which I am a member. My community, however, is being held together by daily chapel and weekly Communion. Sometimes I hear sermons addressing personal and corporate losses and an acknowledgment before God that being in transition is painful and uncertain. Those leading us in worship invite us to lament the losses that have touched our lives. Through song, word, and sacrament, we are voicing the sadness and sorrow we are carrying and the gratitude we experience.

But some things in our community have not changed. The community kitchen, which provides meals for up to a hundred persons a day, has been a silent but stable presence amidst all the change that has occurred. Partnering with other Gospel communities in the neighborhood, the seminary provides meals and take-home food to those in need. The community kitchen is not a place for evangelizing the guests, but all people are served with the love of God. *Do we draw on the silent witness of the community kitchen?* What can the guests of the community kitchen teach us about being a Gospel community?

One ritual I often engage in is having breakfast with brothers and sisters in ministry. Many of the cases written here I received at these breakfasts (though I have changed names and circumstances to protect identities). One of the losses that occurred in writing this book was that these special times ended. Rather than dining with people, I spent the first few hours of every day in research and writing. Although the project has been life-giving and affirming of my call, this is my story. Ministry remains an isolating experience, whether your ministry is being a leader in a congregation or whether your Gospel community is a seminary.

AN OVERVIEW

The first chapter, called "Grieving is the Gospel," identifies ministry as grief work in primarily two ways. Inwardly, you as a leader in your Gospel community need to mourn disappointments and letdowns experienced in your ministry. Sometimes people abandon you and other times your dreams for the congregation end as if you suddenly woke up. Outwardly, your congregation is grieving some loss or change. The good news is that God calls out leaders like you who can be responsive to your own grief and facilitative of your Gospel community's mourning. The gospel or good news in grieving is the promise of new self-understanding and revitalization that is unlocked by doing the work of mourning.

In the chapter called "All the church's losses, all the church's griefs," I provide a framework by which you can recognize the diverse ways in which loss shows its face in your community. I name six losses common to most Gospel communities. In addition, this chapter describes the dynamics that are unleashed by your congregation's experience of loss. By being attentive to these manifestations of grief, you prepare yourself and your congregation to do the work of mourning while avoiding the pitfalls of leading a congregation beyond their grief.

The third chapter, "Conversation-as-the-work-of-mourning," describes the first intentional step in doing the work of mourning. The chapter aims at empowering you to facilitate conversation around the losses and changes that occurred in your congregation, thereby creating the space for your community-as-a-whole to do the work of mourning. The chapter shows formal and informal conversations within your congregation as lifegiving to the community. You will be encouraged to be curious about the stories that individuals can tell about themselves or about the congregation. The body of Christ needs to tell about its past, its present, and its future before a vision of the future can become reality.

Building upon the foundation of numerous conversations with individuals and groups, the fourth chapter nominates Sunday morning worship as a crucial event in facilitating the work of mourning in your congregation. "Communion-as-the-work-of-mourning" reveals how a worship experience can create the space for the work of mourning to occur. The elements within a worship service, ranging from the sermon to singing to serving communion, can invite your community to remember its past as it lives into a new identity. The work of mourning intensifies when our losses are named in the presence of God. A worship experience can become a truth-telling experience similar to that which we see within the Book of Lamentations and Psalms of Lament. These books give us a language of pain, fear, uncertainty, sadness, and sorrow, but also of gratitude and hope—a language seldom heard in sermons or in the music we use in worship.

The final chapter, "Compassion-as-the-work-of-mourning," identifies compassionate ministries as important for two reasons: First, it further facilitates the work of mourning in your congregation, and second, it leads to revitalization. The good news when doing the work of mourning is that your congregation will receive a new self-understanding of what it means to be the body of Christ at this time and in its specific context. Compassionate ministries help your congregation to live into a new identity. It concretizes much conversation about a past, a present, and a future.

CONCLUSION

Loss within Gospel communities is often an overlooked fact. If you as a leader in your congregation are sensitized to the prevalence of loss in your congregation, you will nurture your own sense of call. In addition, you will recognize the diverse losses your community experiences and the impact of those losses on the spiritual and relational well-being of the congregation you serve.

Peter Scazzero, a pastor of a large multinational congregation in Queens, New York, states that health in a congregation depends upon the community's ability to "look below the surface" and to "embrace grieving and loss."[6] Although *When Steeples Cry* does not endorse a medical model of thinking about a congregation, Scazzero does offer insights that can assist us in doing the work of mourning. The vision Scazzero has for us is that of an iceberg, with 90 percent of it submerged below the surface. He challenges us to frequently take careful inventory of what is really going on in our personal and corporate lives and encourages mindfulness and awareness to move beyond self-absorbed introspection.

Scazzero also writes: "In emotionally healthy congregations, people embrace grief as a way to become like God. . . . Why? It is the only pathway to becoming a compassionate person like our Lord Jesus."[7] Scazzero states that for many years he hid his personal losses at the cost of his own well-being and his effectiveness in ministry. The unresolved losses of our lives keep us from walking freely with God and with others. When we mourn, however, we embark upon a journey that leads to spiritual and emotional maturity. *When Steeples Cry* follows Scazzero in identifying the importance of Psalms of Lament in facilitating the work of mourning. Jesus, "the man of sorrows" (Isa. 53:3), beckons us to look at the losses we carry and our congregations experience. This can be confusing, as Scazzero states, since grieving takes us into the "in-between" world of what is present and what is yet to come. The "in-between" world of faith and mourning is a creative space that invites new life.

When Steeples Cry wants to create space for you as you live into your call and for your congregation as they are the bearers of good news. A treasured memory of growing up in Africa comes to mind. Not too far from my childhood home is the Addo Elephant National Park, where a unique herd of African pachyderms roams. Elephants are very sensitive to the experience of loss and are well known to mourn and grieve the death of a member of the herd or when forced relocation separates the herd. As an eleven year old, I remember being impressed by the electrified steel cable fence that kept the elephants separated from orange orchards.

Despite the electrified fence, elephants, primarily young bulls, would break out to invade the adjacent farms. Initially, people thought that these elephants broke out to eat the oranges. It took one person who did a careful study to find that it was not the allure of oranges that caused the elephants to break out. Rather, the behavior was brought about by two reasons: First, the National Parks Board killed the old bulls in an attempt to keep the population numbers down. But elephants are hierarchical animals, and the young bulls needed to be kept in place by the mature bulls. Next, the researcher found that Addo Elephant National Park was overpopulated. Over the years the elephant herd grew, and the young bulls broke loose to claim a piece of land for themselves. Officials stopped killing the old bulls and bought adjacent land. The elephants no longer break out since they have the space to roam freely.

With *When Steeples Cry* I want to create space where the work of mourning can occur. I envision and invite an intentional process of mourning, something that is "unnatural" for many Gospel communities. The space created through having conversation, worshiping together, and engaging in compassionate acts keeps the dynamics unleashed by loss and change from negatively influencing the body of Christ. Ministry defined as such keeps the grief from breaking out. Unaddressed, the dynamics of loss will undo any restoration and revitalization you prayed for and which God granted your congregation.

CHAPTER ONE

Grieving is the gospel

*To be a minister is to know the most searing grief and aban-
donment, daily and profoundly. To be a minister is to make an
all-out, prodigal commitment to a people who cannot possibly
sustain it.*

James Dittes

A S A PASTORAL LEADER IN YOUR CONGREGATION, disappointment, loss, and abandonment are your intimate enemies. For
many of us, the loss we experience daily in ministry is not a
new experience. We first experienced significant loss in our families of
origin, now only to be re-experiencing it in our church families. It cannot be any different, for Scripture describes Christ's church as a prodigal people, unable to follow their Leader and their leaders. A Gospel
community often makes commitments it cannot keep, and when those
commitments are made in a covenant relationship with a pastor, often
it is the pastor who experiences the disappointment and disillusionment. Though these letdowns in ministry are inevitable, what needs to
become certain is both you and your community's ability to grieve
these disappointments for your call and ministry to remain vital and
for your congregation to thrive. The denial of grief greatly undermines
the emotional, spiritual, and relational health of pastoral leaders and
of Gospel communities.

Pastor Peter had a vision for his Gospel community to have a thriving small-group ministry. That this vision coincided with his anticipation of retirement, and thoughts of what he will leave behind in his
community did not go unnoticed. He did all the planning and rallied
a group of eight faithful leaders to be facilitators of the small groups.

Two years after Pastor Peter started planting his vision towards small groups, and one year after the training of the leaders started, the small groups were announced during worship. Fewer people than he'd hoped signed up. He wondered what he could have done differently. Even before the first groups met, two of the facilitators, persons with whom Pastor Peter invested so much time, discerned that their life situations had changed and that they could not take on the added responsibilities of being small-group leaders. Pastor Peter responded by saying he understood and that their past year together had been good. But in fact he was disappointed and angry at the people who opted out, angry at the community for not seeing this as an opportunity to grow in the Lord, and angry at God for placing this vision on his heart. Here, a few years before his retirement, Pastor Peter is grieving silently, in isolation, and does not show or share his disappointment.

Ministry is grief work for church leaders. Yet this kind of grief work reflects only one kind of mourning that occurs in Gospel communities. Most, if not all communities, are grieving! Middlebush Congregational Church has grown from 200 families to about 450 families as farmland is replaced by large single-family homes and apartment developments. The growth in the past three years has been exciting, but it reminds the "old folk" of the loss Middlebush is experiencing. No longer are all the families acquainted with one another, as some members remind Pastor Sharon often. In addition, the "new folk" bring no awareness of the history and traditions of Middlebush, and some are asking for a different style of worship, new mission projects, and other changes. Pastor Sharon says that she is reluctant to praise God from the pulpit for the new people who join their community. She knows that some members of the community would rather not have "them" there.

What kind of leader can empower a Gospel community to grieve and mourn the losses the congregation is experiencing? Surely it has to be persons who can recognize, name, and grieve their own losses first, so that they can be available to their congregation's grief. If loss can cause one to be heartbroken, the metaphor of having a sacred heart affirms leaders of Gospel communities who want to remain responsible and faithful to the communities they serve. "Sacred heart" is a metaphor we receive from the Roman Catholic tradition, and we will revisit the metaphor later in this chapter. A sacred-heart leader is a person who has personal experience in mourning and who is not afraid to walk towards his or her losses. However, it is also a leader who, with empathic sensitivity, can lead a Gospel community to have the very conversations the community wants to avoid. Far from being pessimistic and melancholic, these leaders know the power that is released in Gospel communities when a community remembers and a new identity is forming.

Among Gospel communities, loss is the great equalizer. Whether a congregation is thriving or slowly dying, whether it is "the same church" it was twenty years ago, or whether the community is a new church start, Gospel communities experience loss in significant ways. By God's grace, grieving is not a "dysfunction," and surely it is not something "pathological." Mourning cannot be viewed or addressed through the lens of the disease model even if loss and grief do place us in a state of dis-ease. Our families, our culture, and the church of Christ, however, often view grieving as if it were something pathological. They have forgotten that grief is the normal reaction of persons and Gospel communities to change.

Ministry, then, is grief work in primarily two ways: You as a pastoral leader grieve disappointments and letdowns experienced in your ministry, and every Gospel community is grieving some loss or change. This is the news about today's ministry. The good news, the gospel, is the calling out of leaders like you who can be responsive to your own grief and facilitate your Gospel community's mourning. The gospel in grieving is the promise of new self-understanding and revitalization that is hidden within doing the work of mourning.

A MINISTER'S GRIEF

Ministry itself has been identified as grief work. In 1979, pastoral theologian James E. Dittes wrote an essay, "Ministry as grief work," that invited ministers to grieve leading a people who cannot follow even though they might say they want to.[8] Whether it is dreams and visions for the Gospel community that never materialize, or whether it is living with the disillusionment that the community will never be a fully responsive partner, pastors are encouraged by Dittes to lament and grieve.

Of course not all pastors embrace those moments of emptiness and the sense of loss that Dittes identifies as inherent to the ministry. Rather, some pastors seek out communities where faith and a sense of community, or even love and justice, seem to be thriving abundantly. In such communities, they believe very little ministry is needed. Other ministers "swallow grief dumbly," as if the grief that they internalize as food will never become poisonous to their bodies and their ministries. Still other pastors swallow grief by "denying the life" that was lived or the significance of the relationship that ended. When deaths go ungrieved, death becomes triumphant. Other pastors, however, "deny the death" by denying the limits and breakdown of their relationships. Many pastors have a strong desire to abstain from doing the work of mourning.

Pastor Angelo always wondered about his call to Stony Lake Church, a community in the Reformed tradition. Established more than 150 years ago, Stony Lake was a prominent Gospel community in a town settled by Europeans. Since the 1970s, however, Stony Lake Church has seen the neighborhood change as migrant laborers settled in town. Three years ago the leaders of Stony Lake Church invited Pastor Angelo to start a Hispanic ministry. Even though there were questions about his education—Pastor Angelo does not hold a Masters of Divinity degree from a North American seminary—he was extended a call.

After the initial "honeymoon" period, Pastor Angelo has become increasingly frustrated that his attempts to give the community eyes to see the spiritual needs of his Hispanic people have been ignored. In particular, he had much conflict with the Gospel community's leaders regarding a worship program for the new ministry, and they could not come to a unified vision. In three years the community has not moved far beyond offering Spanish and English as a Second Language classes. A small group of Hispanic believers had fellowship alongside the existing community, but that was all.

After much disagreement, Pastor Angelo left to join the staff at a large Hispanic ministry. His parting thoughts were that it had been a good experiment, but that the congregation was "not ready" for a

Hispanic ministry. Church members defended themselves against this loss by murmuring that Pastor Angelo did not have the right academic credentials for them as a community and that maybe "it was not God's will." Relationships ended and dreams and visions were denied. In Gospel communities, the lives that were lived are often denied as are the endings and deaths of all kinds that occur.

Without a conscious attempt to engage grief in ministry, pastors and leaders in the community have to rely upon many mechanisms to cope with their grief. Some pastors go through the motions of ministry life casually, unable or uninterested in generating any change in their ministries. Some leaders cling tenaciously to their visions, unable to hear the "no" they receive from the Gospel community. Some pastors leave their Gospel community to take their visions elsewhere, blaming and shaming their previous congregation for not being spiritually mature enough to live into the pastor's vision. In ministry, Dittes writes, few pastors seek out the struggling, difficult-to-work-with but "faithful remnant," which promises the maximum possibility for ministry. Some pastors minimize the seriousness of a partnership that cannot be trusted and the loss it caused while they swallow their grief, keeping it private, personal, and ignored.

GOD IS A GOD OF PATHOS

There are ministers who indeed do grief work. This "work" is anchored in a God who knows the grief caused by loss, most particularly the grief from being abandoned by God's people. It is anchored in Jesus, who experienced the rejection, isolation, and wrath of God: "My God, my God, why have you forsaken me?" (Matt. 27:46). Jesus, who cried bitterly at the death of his friend Lazarus (John 11:35), or who became troubled when he knew his death was imminent (John 13:21), invites you to mourn your losses.

Events and human actions arouse in God joy or sorrow, pleasure or wrath. As the Jewish scholar Abraham J. Heschel writes, God is a God of pathos, a God of loving care who has concern for humanity, whether it is from a pathos of love or a pathos of anger.[9] God is pathetic! There is nothing stoic or pietistic about God. In God's divine freedom, God is involved in and can react to human history. Surely the fact that ministry is grief work must affect God, who enters into a covenantal relationship with us. If the grief of God is a central theme in the Noah account (Gen. 6–9), then grief must be an emotion God experiences when God thinks about today's Gospel communities. *How do you think God is viewing your ministry and congregation?* Is God grieving for you? Is God grieving for what is happening to and in your community?

Pastoral leaders and Gospel communities have cause for hope in their grief because they can remember God being faithful to them throughout their history. Whether present through a cloud by day, a pillar of fire by night, or the blessing of God's Spirit, we can remind ourselves that God is present in our mourning. Sometimes it may be difficult to believe that it is possible to experience God's presence. In such moments we might need to rely on the testimony of our spiritual ancestors in Scripture or our contemporary friends or perhaps even a favorite author. With God present in our losses, mourning becomes a creative force that not only heals, restores, and revitalizes, but also anticipates a new future. When grieving does not occur, however, the opposite is true. Then grief becomes a literal black hole devouring the spiritual and relational energy within the Gospel community. Grieving can bring hope as grief can bring despair.

In classic Greek, there is only one word to describe both poison and antidote, sickness and cure: *pharmakon*. The origins and function of the word *pharmacy* can be traced to this ancient word. Any substance capable of causing a very good or very bad action, according to the circumstances and the dosage, can be a pharmakon. The pharmakon was seen by the Greeks as a magic drug or as a volatile elixir, and as philosopher and literary scholar René Girard argues, its administration had best be left in the hands of those who enjoy special knowledge and exceptional powers—priests, magicians, shamans, and doctors.[10] Even as late as fifth-century Greek culture, a culture that scapegoated individuals to assure the "health" of the larger community, the pharmakon referred to the scapegoat whose life was symbolically linked to death and resurrection. The pharmakos (in this case, the scapegoat) thus became a pharmakon (the antidote) to the society.

For you and your community, loss and mourning can either be poison or the good news of life restored, depending on how the work of grieving is done. Grieving can be a creative healing power if the dreams that died are not denied; when the relationships that disappointed are mourned but not abandoned; when the frustrations and failed expectations of ministry are honored. Not grieving, however, can become poison to the body of Christ, leaving it vulnerable. Grief then can linger into deeper sadness, hostility, paralysis, resistance to change, and even apathy. It is estimated that between twelve- to fifteen-hundred pastors leave the ministry every month and some Gospel communities literally die, closing their doors forever.

Grieving communities need ministers and church leaders, persons who carry special knowledge and who are seen by society as being exceptional, to facilitate the congregation's mourning. *If you as a leader of your Gospel community do not become responsive to your community's reaction to change, who will?* Dittes's 1979 essay beckons ministers to re-call their ministry of grief, to deepen, reform, refresh, and redirect that ministry, thereby working through the grief that befalls every Gospel community. Pastors, for example, need not take the "rejections" personally, since many of the resistances in a community are fueled by uncertainty and lack of empowerment, aspects of congregational life that pastors can address. Like a dance with two dance partners, the minister often discovers that her partner is out of step. Those moments become moments of grief to be experienced fully. When you grieve the disappointments and disillusionments you experience in ministry, you create space for yourself to continue to grow in ministry. Such space in turn makes growth for your congregation possible. This task, the art of creating space for others to grow, Dittes identifies as the essence of pastoral ministry.

GRIEVING IS THE GOSPEL IN GOSPEL COMMUNITIES

Pastoral theologians especially have been sensitive to the loss and mourning clergy experience in ministry. Making oneself available to listen to the stories of pastors will bring such sensitivity. Surely, sensitivity to loss and mourning is needed to recognize the loss and mourning within Gospel communities. As stated in the Introduction, most mainline Protestant denominations and many Gospel communities experience membership loss of between 0.5–1.0 percent annually.

The narratives of many congregations are tainted by loss. For some communities, especially congregations with a historic ethnic identity, membership loss has been an intimate enemy for more than forty years. Not only are ministers experiencing loss (and called upon to grieve), but communities also are grieving and are in need of mourning. Examples of Gospel communities who grieve a loss or numerous losses, who are growing at a rapid rate, who remember a time that was, who are uncertain as to who they are, or communities that recognize that today is not the same as yesterday and requires a new way of being, such Gospel communities crowd the ecclesiastical landscape. Of course, these different scenarios are not mutually exclusive. *What is happening to the community you are leading?*

- Three Rivers Congregational Church, a United Church of Christ ministry, is a community that knows loss and abandonment intimately. "Three Rivers," as the congregation is affectionately called, is a suburban Gospel community that once had a membership list of more than 600 families. Two full-time pastors served a congregation that now registers only 125 "families." Pastor Beth has been their only pastor the past four years. The majority of the congregation is retired and widowed persons. As "Three Rivers" witnessed a decline in membership, the number of people in the neighborhood increased about fifteen-fold.

  Pastor Beth was surprised when she discovered that the average age of her congregants was fifty-eight. Many of the older community members nostalgically recall confirmation classes of up to sixty strong. They often refer to Pastor Paul, Pastor Beth's predecessor, who served the community as the senior pastor for twenty-seven years before he suddenly died of a heart attack. In addition, Pastor Beth is often told about people she has never met. Pastor Beth is frustrated with her community. Although they are financially secure, thanks in part to an endowment fund started by Pastor Paul, every effort she has made to initiate intimacy and personal relationships has failed. It is as if the Gospel community has lost its capacity for mutuality and hospitality. Instead, the church members prefer to live in the past.

- Seven years ago, according to Pastor Gerhard, St. Luke Lutheran Church "had more money than we knew what to do with." With the economic downturn of recent years, however, his community saw how the finances went from being robust to being busted. The Gospel community withdrew some of their support to mission projects around the world and is concerned that they will not be able to afford the much-needed renovations to their church building. At a recent board of elders meeting, someone made a cynical remark regarding the paint that is peeling in the sanctuary. Despite having financial concerns, St. Luke's members are committed to the life of their congregation. Though they made the difficult decision to withhold denominational monies, they did make a commitment to reach out into their community.

  The finance committee, however, remains aware of their "desperate" financial situation. The members of St. Luke's are reminded monthly by the finance committee where the congregation stands vis-à-vis the approved budget. Some say that the primary gifts the church leaders are interested in are the members' material gifts. Leadership of Gospel communities is on dangerous ground when the primary relationship they have with the members of their communities is an "economic relationship." At a recent congregational meeting, the community had a heated debate—some called it an argument—that lasted almost an hour. Members disagreed whether they should increase by $600 a month the rent on a building the community owns. A member of the community remarked that the conversation is about $7,200 returns in rental income; she had her doubts that this $7,200 will "save" them. However, the debate continued. The loss of material possessions can bring significant anxiety to a Gospel community. But how does one mourn the loss of material possessions? And is it appropriate for a Christian community to mourn the loss of material possessions at the same time as being taught not to become attached to worldly things?

- Unlike St. Luke Lutheran Church, who lost material possessions, First Presbyterian Church has lost part of its identity. Ask the members of the community where they worship, and one most likely will get the answer: "I belong to the Steeple Church." First Presbyterian is like many other Gospel communities in cities that have celebrated their one-hundredth anniversary. Once the largest congregation a few blocks removed from the inner city, the community is now caught in that area between the inner city and suburbia, an area where many formerly majestic homes are in dilapidated condition and where minority groups form the majority of the neighborhood. In recent years, members have been asking what happened to the community once heralded as an example in the denomination, a tower offering guidance to many other Gospel communities. First Presbyterian realized that its future existence was uncertain. The majority of the members commuted more than fifteen minutes to come to worship, giving them little stake in the community's neighborhood. The members had to admit that they were a "tall steeple church" at one time. Somewhere along the line, however, they lost the image that communicates an identity of being a leader in their denomination and society.

But the community wants to be "The Steeple Church" again. The members have realized that to reclaim this image, they will need to bridge the gap between the Gospel community they want to be and the community they currently are. Church membership has stabilized, they are meeting their budget, and a new sense of hope has entered as community events are hosted in their building. Recently, however, conflict has entered the Gospel community. Some called it a "worship war" as the members struggle to discern whether they should introduce a contemporary or even a Spanish worship service. Others say that all the community needs is a "preaching pastor," suggesting that good preaching will bring new life and lives to the community. A new group of voices wondered out loud whether the community should not relocate to a large piece of land next to an interstate, believing that "if we build it, they will come." This latter group believes First Presbyterian can be the fastest growing Protestant congregation in North America by the year 2015. The community can be a "tall steeple church" again.

- Wild River Church has been a community church since its first days in 1861. It was a natural decision that the congregation would be the host for numerous community events in town. In recent years, however, Alcoholics Anonymous is the only community group that makes use of the church building. Pastor Armstrong remembers the letter the Gospel community received eight years ago in which the township informed the community that the traditional Memorial Day celebrations will not conclude with a worship service in their building, but rather with an ecumenical service to be conducted at the town's civic center. The letter also asked Pastor Armstrong whether he would continue to be the marshal of the Memorial Day parade. He states with sarcastic humor that the "anonymous" in Alcoholics Anonymous aptly describes his community.

  Wild River Church seems to have little to offer the people in town. The congregation's teenagers find driving, smoking, tattooing, and binge drinking rites of passage; couples favor the golf club's new clubhouse as a place in which to get married; and the funeral home has become almost exclusively the place where funeral services are being held. These changes have brought self-doubt to the Gospel community—Who are we?—to which the congregation has responded by rigidly holding on to their traditions. As the Gospel community's teens join the local Vineyard Congregation, the members chastise themselves saying that their youth drifts off because they as parents and adults were lax about inculcating them with their responsibilities towards their faith tradition.

- Elder Van Wyck would be able to resonate with the experience of Wild River Episcopal Church. She summarized the dilemma Voorhees Reformed Church (VRC) is experiencing when she reflected on her community and her town, and said: "But then they built the mall down the road." She clarified her statement, saying that "VRC was the center of this historic Dutch community, with the Post Office next to the church buildings . . . but then they built the mall down the road." Elder Van Wyck refers to a strip mall that was built twelve years ago, which includes a liquor store, a bakery, and numerous smaller, private businesses. These stores were later joined by a Barnes and Noble bookstore. She can name the day, almost the moment, when Voorhees Reformed Church lost a privileged position within the community to be "relocated" on the periphery of their society. People now drive right past the church on Sunday mornings to buy fresh bread and bagels at the food store or have breakfast and read their newspaper at Barnes and Noble. Since that day, Voorhees Reformed Church has searched for ways to recapture the central position in the community that she lost.

VRC has attempted numerous events to break its isolation within the community. However, they had to admit that their Fish Fry could not compete with fast-food operations and other restaurants in town. Likewise, their community auction was not the success they had prayed for. With nostalgic clarity, Elder Van Wyck envisions a future when Voorhees Reformed Church will again be the heart of the community. Her silent fear, however, is that the congregation will close its doors just as she has seen other churches in the community do.

As is true of all losses, whether in the lives of individuals or in Gospel communities, some were avoidable and others were not. Some of the losses are temporary losses, but the majority are permanent in nature. Some of the losses are actual while a few may only be imagined. Some of the losses were anticipated, while others surprised everyone. Some of the losses were tangible and others were intangible. And some of the losses were due to being left behind, while others were due to leaving. Regardless of the cause, it is clear that all Gospel communities, whether experiencing a declining membership or a growing membership, experience losses of all kinds. *Not only ministers know intense disappointments and mourning, but their ministries too are grieving with the diversity the body of Christ brings.* Pastoral leaders and their congregations need to do grief work. The next chapter, which offers a systematic framework to identify loss in Gospel communities, will empower you to help your congregation name and identify its losses.

The persons essential to the grieving process in any Gospel community are the leaders. Within the Protestant tradition, it is thus the pastor(s), the elders, the deacons, and other lay leaders who hold the responsibility for assisting the community in its grief work. Since grieving needs to occur in an organic way, from the inside out and from the bottom up, congregational and denominational leadership cannot announce a new program that will allow individual congregations to grieve or thrive. Programmatic mourning "from above" is bound to fail, thereby becoming another loss the community experiences. Rather, if leaders of Gospel communities grieve the losses they have experienced as individuals, and lead by example, they can create the space needed for their faith community to do its work of mourning. For steeples that cry, a certain kind of leader is needed—a person who recognizes that mourning can facilitate the revitalization of the body of Christ. Mourning is an antidote!

LEADING WHEN GRIEVING IS THE GOSPEL

It is important that you as a church leader are able to mourn and grieve. If grief is the news of the moment, ministry implies significant grief work for you as a leader of a Gospel community. In addition, congregations need leaders that can help them grieve, since loss is a common experience for all Gospel communities, whether it is an unwanted loss or a loss created through dynamic leaders as a ministry grows and expands. Mourning, of course, is difficult, for life has taught few of us that the work of mourning is good news!

Even though their suits may not project an image of pastoral sensitivity, it is business leaders who are at the forefront of pastoral awareness. Ronald Heifetz and Marty Linsky, consultants and professors at the John F. Kennedy School of Government at Harvard University, published a book that includes grieving as a trait that leaders need to develop. In *Leadership on the Line: Staying Alive Through the Dangers of Leading* (2002), they write that leaders need to help those who follow them to grieve, for "people do not resist change per se. People resist loss."[11] Drawing on their experiences with leaders in politics, the business world, and in academic and religious institutions, Heifetz and Linsky identify loss and the grieving it requires as a central task of effective leadership.

It might seem odd to mention a contribution from the corporate world in a chapter stating that news coming from many congregations includes reports of grieving and mourning. But Heifetz and Linsky identify the healing power in grieving and they encourage leaders to facilitate grieving in a positive and nonpathological manner. I wrote this book to empower you by giving you a framework for identifying, naming, and grieving losses. It is not my goal to expose dysfunction in congregational life. Grief is not pathological, even though the symptoms of grief can cause a person or a congregation to lapse into dysfunction. Rather, this book provides a framework to understand a very normal and universal congregational experience. Congregations, by God's grace, survive losses, but a grieving community might not thrive, whether spiritually, emotionally, or relationally, if the work of mourning is not being done.

The modern paradigm for leadership as described by Heifetz and Linsky makes a clear distinction between technical problems and adaptive challenges. Technical problems are those for which we already know the solutions. Some problems, however, are not amenable to authoritative expertise or standard operating procedures. Someone who provides answers from on high cannot solve adaptive challenges, for adaptive challenges require experiments, new discoveries, and adjustments by many people and from numerous places in the organization or community.

Grieving a loss is an adaptive challenge. As with other adaptive challenges such as experiencing conflict, rapid growth and expansion, or deciding on the pace of initiating change, the process of grieving and mourning does not give people a guarantee at the beginning of the process that the outcome will be any better than the current position. Furthermore, not everybody will be convinced that grieving can be good news to their Gospel community, the antidote to painful and even "forgotten" experiences. *How can you envision yourself as an adaptive leader who can lead your community to discover the power within mourning?*

As an adaptive challenge, loss does not require authorities who have the drive to fix, but rather it seeks empowered people who can learn new ways of grieving and being together. Furthermore, we in leadership do not lead the community into areas we do not or cannot go in our personal or family lives. The adaptive challenge of grieving, of course, confronts any book such as *When Steeples Cry*. If the book is experienced as a "how-to" book but does not succeed in empowering you to mourn and grieve personal losses and lead with sensitivity to the pervasiveness of loss, no revitalization will occur. You will not be revitalized, nor will your community receive new life.

Heifetz and Linsky state that systemic dysfunction typically sets in when an adaptive challenge is addressed as if it is a technical problem. They have witnessed this mistake in leaders serving various organizations: public, private, and ecclesial. This word of caution is especially important for the grieving body of Christ in North America, where a programmatic attitude has invaded the ecclesiastical mind. One Gospel community responded to its membership loss by announcing an aggressive program of church growth, church revitalization, and church planting. This program is even seen as a "natural" process! The denominational leadership seem ignorant to the fact that losses cannot be replaced and that the experience of loss is natural when change occurs. Losses can only be mourned. In addition, a new church plant typically has a character that is nontraditional, thereby adding to the community's difficulty to settle on a congregational and denominational identity.

In their first chapter, entitled "The heart of danger," Heifetz and Linsky identify loss as a central crisis or danger for today's leaders. They point to loss even though effective leaders often facilitate growth and new life. To reach a new position of growth and revitalization, people have to be persuaded to give up the love they know for a love they've never experienced. People need to be empowered to take a leap of faith in themselves, in life, and with their God. The people will experience the loss of a relationship that, despite its problems, provides satisfaction and familiarity, and they will suffer the discomfort or sustained uncertainty about what will replace it. Breaking with the past comes at a cost and a sense of disloyalty to the sources of the values that formed the past. *How will the ministry of the beloved previous pastor be seen if a congregation has to admit that they were never empowered to identify, name, and grieve losses?*

"A leap of faith" is appropriate language to use in Gospel communities! Will a pastor have the faith to address her personal losses? Will she have the faith to lead and empower her community in identifying, naming, and grieving the losses the community experienced or are experiencing? Will a pastor have the faith to ask the Gospel community about what they are leaving behind even as they journey with God into an unknown future? Faith might be what is needed when one experiences any change that challenges the very identity or self-definition of oneself or the community. Surely a pastor will need faith to live with the guilt feelings he might experience knowing that his acts of leadership cause loss in the lives of those around him. Effective leadership makes one an unfamiliar guest in one's own home.

Thus, a leader who leads only by clarifying the vision of a new future and an acknowledgment that it is a difficult process for the community will fail. Pointing to a hopeful future is not enough! Rather, the specific losses along the way have to be named and grieved. Heifetz and Linsky write that those being led need to know that you, as their leader, know what you are asking them to give up on the way to creating a better future. Effective leaders will grieve with the community and will memorialize the loss in a tangible manner with the community. Sermons and worship can be used to envision not only the future, but also to grieve the losses in a tangible manner through ritualization.

THE EGYPT TABLE

Pastor Lou started a ten-week sermon series on the Exodus narrative, asking whether the Gospel community can learn from Israel as Israel left Egypt. In the series, he named the places the community had been in its eighty years of being a congregation. He identified previous pastors and prominent members who helped build the congregation. He stepped away from the pulpit and placed name plates of those individuals on the now-empty seats, then proceeded with his sermon. He recounted significant events, such as the different anniversaries the community experienced. He showed pictures of the fellowship hall that burned down and described memorable potlucks that were eaten in the building. He invited others to bring photos of past church events and gatherings to worship, and while singing "Our God, our help in ages past," the photos and other artifacts were placed on a memory table in the corner of the sanctuary. Some called it "The

Egypt Table." Often, Pastor Lou acknowledged God's faithfulness to this body of believers while asking open-ended questions about their future. During a communion service, a feast of "remembrance and of hope," he remembered not only Christ's sacrifice, but also paused to remember God's past with the Gospel community. All along, Pastor Lou is remembering the future with his community.

Adaptive challenges are best addressed in "holding environments," Heifetz and Linsky write. This therapeutic construct can be defined as the space created by a network of relationships within which people can tackle difficult and even divisive questions without flying apart. Within the holding environment one can address not only the difficulties that are experienced, but also the new difficulties that are created as one addresses the hurdles that are impinging upon a community.

In some contexts the holding environment will be a physical space, such as a retreat center; in others it will be a shared language or a communal history. Other communities may have their holding environment determined by a deep sense of trust in their leaders or by faith in their tradition. However, one aspect common to all holding environments is effective leaders who create relationships that can withstand much strain and anxiety before the relationships break down. Creating such a space is not only a difficult task; it can be dangerous, for it often leads the community into uncharted territory.

Pastor Lou created a holding environment for his congregation by inviting conversation about the community's past and its future. While some members of the Gospel community spread rumors questioning Pastor Lou's leadership and decision to reflect on the past, Pastor Lou remained surprised at how many people would bring artifacts, pictures, and even handwritten notes to "The Egypt Table" during worship and even at other times. He had to resist becoming reactive to the rumors that reflecting on the past is "a waste of time," and processed his hurt with a few caring friends. This group of colleagues in turn became a holding environment for him. In addition, Pastor Lou had to slow down the group within the congregation who wanted to move forward at a pace that would leave the process of grieving at risk. His knowledge of systems thinking convinced him of the importance of paying close attention to the emotional process within his community.

Of course, the ability to create a holding environment is a gift you have received to some extent. Not all leaders are equally gifted in this regard! As an art, however, creating a holding environment is a skill that you can learn. *Can you admit that you might be an apprentice in creating the holding environment that allows Gospel communities to mourn and move beyond their grief?* Can you become excited as you continue to grow in your ability to create a holding environment? If the adaptive challenge of loss is an essential task of leadership, one's ability to create a holding environment is all important.

Leadership on the Line discusses many aspects of leadership that will be instructive for a minister who addresses the adaptive challenge of loss in a Gospel community: conflict management, pacing the work being done, empowering all involved to do the work they have to do, how to intervene if necessary, how to hold steady if resentment settles in, and more. Three characteristics, however, are central to leading Gospel communities: innocence, curiosity, and compassion. These characteristics, Heifetz and Linsky state, can be found in someone who has a sacred heart.

"Sacred Heart" is the title of the final chapter in *Leadership on the Line*. A leader with a sacred heart portrays aliveness and childlike innocence. With playful creativity they think ingenious thoughts to get others unstuck. In doing so, one can become strange to one's community without becoming a stranger. The minister as a lonely outsider returns to be the pivotal figure in the community as the community moves into new visions and realities.

+ + +

A POWERFUL SERMON GROUP

Pastor Sharon used her creativity to welcome new members of Middlebush Congregational Church to the Gospel community. This congregation is growing at a rapid pace. As she listened to the "old folk" complaining that they did not know everybody, she decided not to be reactive to their comments. Rather, she invited the Gospel community to be in one of four sermon groups with her. Half of the sermon group consisted of "old folk." Much of the time in the sermon group was spent sharing how the members' stories relate to the sermon text. Not only did the sermon group members receive the opportunity to enter into significant relationships with one another, they also assisted Pastor Sharon in preparing her sermons. In addition, Pastor Sharon made a point of introducing the sermon group to the congregation each week. Subsequently, she has heard that some of the "old folk" are inviting newer members in the sermon group to dinner.

+ + +

Besides a sense of aliveness and innocence, you need a sense of curiosity as you become aware of the losses your community experiences. Curiosity here means a sense of continual growth without succumbing to an assuredness that exudes over-confidence. When you address adaptive challenges, questions about your competence will be raised in the short term. However, you will gain the trust of those you lead. In a culture where "rights" and "wrongs" have been ingrained in our minds since childhood and where layers of self-justification protect us, keeping the mind curious is not easy. A curious mind learns to listen, hears, and thinks new and often disturbing thoughts. It is a mind that keeps asking the difficult questions, about loss, anger, resistance, and much more.

+ + +

CURIOUS ABOUT AN IMAGE

The leadership team of First Presbyterian Church, "the Steeple Church," had a well-developed sense of curiosity. First, they spent much time inquiring where the image of a "Steeple Church" came from. Early in the community's history, the steeple was the highest point in town. However, their imagination led them beyond this obvious explanation or "easy answer." They asked when the image was first used; how previous pastors and leaders built the image; about the relationship between the congregation's witness and the image; when the image began to lose its "shine"; and what would it mean to the community to reclaim that image. As leaders they asked whether there is something "towering" about them—whether they have the gifts, resources, and commitment to be fruitful as a congregation at this time. Some members in the leadership team lost patience with the process and resigned. New leaders stepped forward with a passionate commitment to First Presbyterian. Curiosity slows down the process of discernment significantly, but it also creates the possibility for imaginative and vital relationships and visions to come forward.

+ + +

The third fundamental characteristic of leaders who lead people through loss is *compassion*. Becoming a co-creator with God, who Abraham J. Heschel refers to as "the most moved mover," implies that you see your parishioners through the eyes of compassion. The longings and aspirations of others are deeply felt by a sacred-heart leader. Obviously, if your heart is closed, you cannot fathom those stakes or the losses people will have to sustain as they conserve what is most precious and learn how to thrive in the new environment you lead them to. Compassion is needed to pay attention to the needs of others when you feel you have no energy left—even for yourself.

+ + +

BECOMING COMPASSIONATE

Pastor Beth, the pastor who serves Three Rivers Congregational Church, is learning how compassion can energize her call. At first, the losses that dominated her mind were the 450 families that disappeared off the members list the past years and Pastor Paul, who suddenly died while serving the community. As she began to look at the losses she has experienced in her life—the biggest being her family that was broken apart when her parents divorced—she saw that her parishioners were grieving personal losses, too. Whereas she previously shied away from talking about loss, she now encourages conversation about painful moments and memories, some pertaining to Three Rivers and others not. She surprised herself when she discovered that listening to other's losses is less draining than listening to the nostalgic (and unconscious) mourning of parishioners. With renewed interest she looks at Jesus, who reached out to people in their need.

+ + +

Heifetz and Linsky identify Jesus as a leader with a sacred heart. They identify Jesus' aliveness, his innocence, curiosity, and his compassion as the very aspects of leadership that should be followed. These traits can never be contained in a "how-to" fashion, as if all that is needed is to follow Jesus' example. Rather, growth in spiritual, relational, and emotional maturity is the only way one can become more alive, be more innocent, and remain curious about God and about life. Jesus did not portray a "closed heart," a way of being that is characterized by the numbing of the self, so that the realities of people's lives are not felt anymore. Closed-heart leaders portray cynicism, arrogance, or callousness. They might be dressed up as being realistic, being authoritarian, and being thick-skinned from all the hurt they received in life and as leaders. Although cynicism can be protective, it removes your sense of being alive and innocent, traits needed by you in order to feel, hear, and identify the joys and sorrows experienced by your Gospel community. God's promises do not keep you out of the fire and the water, but God remains a constant companion with you in the fire and the water. Having a sacred heart allows you to be the minister that can do grief work for yourself as you empower others to do their grief work.

How does your innocence, curiosity, and compassion come forward as you engage ministry as grief work? These traits are important to any adaptive challenge you want to address, for without these traits, you might see the problem as a technical problem that you can solve by announcing a new reality. Loss cannot be addressed through aggressive programs of church growth or church management. Having a sacred heart will sustain you through the disillusions of ministry and the losses ministry brings to you. It will assist you in recognizing the pervasiveness of loss in your Gospel community.

GRIEF WORKERS ARE PROPHETS BRINGING (GOOD) NEWS

Cultivating the skill or art needed to identify, name and grieve the losses of ministry is a gift from God. It is to become a prophet, for the prophets were persons who felt passionately; who became preoccupied with trivialities, who communicated in emotional and imaginative yet concrete language, and who brought hope through their message of compassion (Abraham Heschel). The prophet is a counselor and a messenger! Surely such a witness is needed not only to identify the losses within the community, but also to lead your congregation beyond the debilitating reach of grief.

Heschel, however, warns that prophets speak one octave too high, making it impossible for the people to hear them. In exposing the loss a community experienced you run the risk of not being heard. Like a Jeremiah of old, you are invited to follow the consciousness of the prophets, whether in their loneliness, their grief, or in the joys of ministry (Jer. 15:15–16).

In the introductory course to pastoral care and counseling I teach, I regularly ask the students during the initial lectures whether they have experienced significant losses in their lives. The vast majority of students report that they have not experienced any significant losses. It seems as if life experiences such as experiencing parents divorcing or moving from one city to another, for example, do not connote loss to these students. The final project required for this course includes a pastoral response to the death of a twelve-year-old boy. After a semester's worth of time and sensitizing students to the pervasiveness of loss and empowerment to become responsive to people in their grief, the students reflect in their papers on many losses they have experienced. Some reflect on how the boy's death reminded them of a classmate who died when they were in school. Others revisit the loss and isolation they felt those times they were left behind. Some students mourn the young boy or girl in them who died when they were sexually molested in their early childhood or teen years. Many students embrace the pervasiveness of loss in their own lives. In every class I discover anew what a privilege it is to be a witness to the birth of sacred hearts!

The birth of the sacred heart is a necessary first step before a leader in a Gospel community can recognize and be sensitive to the losses the body of Christ experienced and is asked to embrace. To move beyond the mere recognition of loss, communal and corporate mourning and grieving depend greatly upon leaders who can grieve and mourn personal losses. Most Gospel communities, if not all, have not developed a sense of communal grieving. Grieving remains foreign—a taboo—to many individuals, families, and Gospel communities.

In this chapter, I argued that for you as a leader of your Gospel community, being in ministry implies grieving many disappointments and disillusionments, both personal and professional. In addition, your congregation is mourning. To address this painful reality in our communities, we need leaders who can name and grieve their own personal losses as they assist and empower their Gospel communities to mourn and grieve. We need leaders with sacred hearts.

Even as I bring loss within Gospel communities into the center of our vision, I remain aware of the danger of reducing every difficulty that a community experiences to the dynamics of loss. Not all the "stuff" that happens in your congregation can be reduced to the dynamics of loss and grief, but the inability to grieve significant losses does influence your congregation adversely.

In the next chapter, I provide a framework that can be used to identify loss within your congregation as the body of Christ. In addition, I discuss three core theories about loss and mourning that can inform our discussion of loss in Gospel communities. First, I look at the contribution of a psychologist, John Bowlby, who names the experience of loss as the only experience common to all people. Loss becomes a motivational force, determining how individuals and congregations relate to themselves, to God, and to the world. As a motivational force, grieving shapes one's imagination. Second, I turn to a psychiatrist, Silvano Arieti, who writes compellingly about the "psychodynamics of sadness" and how a response to loss can be placed on a continuum that leads from mild sadness to severe depression. Arieti argues that sadness prompts the desire for a dominant and powerful person or entity to miraculously change "the way it is." A pastor, a specific program, or even God can become the dominant other to a Gospel community who experienced losses and who are longing for revitalization. Lastly, psychotherapist Susan Roos introduces the concept of "chronic sorrow" as the normal process of grieving that occurs if there is perpetual loss. Whether the body of Christ is growing or not, grief and loss are fundamental to being a Gospel community.

CHAPTER TWO

All the church's losses, All the church's griefs

Grief is like a bomber circling round and dropping its bombs each time the circle brings it overhead. . . . For in grief nothing "stays put." One keeps on emerging from a phase, but it always recurs. Round and round. Everything repeats.

C. S. Lewis

L IKE MOST LEADERS, you probably want to know whether the dynamics of grief have entered your Gospel community and, if so, find reasons for the losses causing the grief. Knowing why the losses occurred carries the illusion that the knowledge will prohibit, diminish, or even remove the grief. It is tempting to seek ways to convince ourselves that the losses experienced are not so invasive, not so important, could not be avoided, and thus should be accepted as "part of life." Sometimes we convince ourselves that the loss can be reversed if we know the reasons for it. An attempt to quantify loss and change—as if the only changes a congregation is experiencing can be contained in numbers—can be a defense against the experience of pain and the confusion loss and change brings. The statistics of membership loss in mainline Protestant denominations tempt us to rationalize the losses Gospel communities experience.

To empower your Gospel community in its grief, however, you have to do more than merely prepare statistics about membership gain or loss, financial surplus or shortfall. Rather, as a leader of a Gospel community, you are called to be sensitive to the pervasiveness of loss in your community as you lead this body of Christ in and through their grief. The Introduction defined grief as *the normal emotional, spiritual, physical, and relational reaction to the experience of loss and change.* Mourning, in contrast, *is the intentional process of letting go of relationships, dreams, visions, and more, as the community lives into a new identity after the experience of loss and change.* The work of mourning is to live through grief; to live with loss and change. Mourning is not about replacement, but rather is a process of defining a new identity. For church leaders called to lead their Gospel communities toward renewal and revitalization or to be faithful and fruitful, mourning losses is of central importance.

Reading this chapter will empower you to recognize the diverse ways in which loss shows its face in your community. Six losses common to most Gospel communities are named, and you will hear how grief manifested in some communities. By being attentive to these manifestations of grief, you can take the first steps to assist your community in doing the work of mourning while avoiding the pitfalls of leading a community in their grief. In the next chapters, I discuss three different paths the work of mourning can take for a Gospel community: conversation, communion (worship), and hospitable compassion.

As we think about the grief Gospel communities experience, the apostle Paul's metaphor of the church as "the body of Christ," which identifies the Christian identity as corporate, can be instructive to us. As embodied persons awaiting our own deaths, we are predisposed to experience change as loss. In the metaphor "the body of Christ," the theological and personal come together. It provides us with a deeper understanding of the nature of a Gospel community. Grief asks that the *ekklesia,* those called out, call upon themselves as they experience loss and change.[12]

THE BODY OF CHRIST

Homer is identified as the first Greek scholar to write about the "body." However, he wrote about it almost exclusively as an individual dead body, a corpse. Thoughts such as his led to the body being experienced as something alien, something outside ourselves. It introduced a discomfort that persists to this day. Thus, it is no surprise that, like the Stoics of old, soul care is often seen as more important than taking care of the body. We need to die beautifully and peacefully, as if it is the last task of life to say that we conquered life and overcame our bodies. Since the ancient Greeks, the body has become mere matter and form. Despite our culture's destructive ways of being body-conscious, we can find inspiration and comfort in the image of the church as the body of Christ.

The New Testament church functions as a body politic (James Dunn). The image and metaphor of "toú somatos toú Christoú" (the body of Christ) is the dominant theological theme in Paul's ecclesiology (See 1 Cor. 10; 12; Rom.7, 12; Col. 1; Eph. 4). For Paul, "the Body of Christ" is inspired by the physical body of Christ, crucified and resurrected, and witnesses to believers' participation in both events through the communion meal. Depending on different pastoral purposes, Paul's phrase can have many meanings: It can refer to the physical body of Christ (crucified or risen), the elements of the Lord's Supper, or an individual congregation. Later the phrase referred to the church of Christ as a whole. The phrase suggests a charismatic community of unity in diversity, where mutuality and interdependence describe interpersonal relationships.[13]

The metaphor of the body of Christ contains significant theological truths, one being the inner unity of a Gospel community under the headship of Christ. However, this anthropomorphic image also communicates that the body of Christ is a cognitive and an affective body. In Romans 12:3, for example, Paul calls upon the body of Christ to "think with sober judgment" about themselves, and proceeds to describe the unity in diversity of many spiritual gifts that is found in the body of Christ. Likewise, the Letter to the Romans suggests that some Gospel communities experience shame (Rom. 1:16b).

Paul's use of the body-metaphor indicates that his writing reflects a wholistic anthropology and an ecclesiology modeled after the human body, always addressing our minds, our emotions, our wills, our souls, and even our bodies. It is therefore no surprise that Gospel communities can experience powerful emotions or emotional states. For example:

- Gospel communities experience dependency on God and Christ as the Head of the Body, interdependency on brothers and sisters in Christ as co-members of one body, and independence as one body separated from the world (1 Cor. 12; Rom. 12).

- As "adoptees," the body of Christ knows the pain of rejection and relinquishment and the joy of experiencing a sense of belonging (Rom. 8:23).
- The Letter to the Corinthians not only beckons the church in Corinth to respect the many parts of the body of Christ (1 Cor. 12:12ff), but also identifies love as a primary affective force within Gospel communities (1 Cor. 13). Love combats emotional experiences such as pride, selfishness, anger, and boastfulness.
- Paul encourages the Colossians to have grateful hearts (Col. 3:16).
- In the Letters to the Philippians and to the Thessalonians, Paul highlights the joy the community can experience, with a sense of peace that flows from that experience.
- The Galatians are admonished to experience hope.
- The Philippians are warned against the danger of anxiety or worry (Phil. 4:6).
- The Thessalonians are encouraged not to grieve as if they had no hope (1 Thess. 4:13ff).
- Throughout Paul's letters, he encourages communities to praise God and act from a position of adoration (Rom. 11:33ff; Eph. 1:3–14).
- In addition, the body of Christ experiences hospitable compassion (2 Cor. 1:3–4).

Though not an exhaustive list of emotional experiences or states the body of Christ can experience, it nonetheless indicates that the church's experience of powerful emotions is central to Scripture's anthropomorphic understanding of the church. One of the many emotions experienced by today's Gospel communities is grief following diverse losses.

Similar to our bodies that have memory, the body of Christ "remembers" emotional experiences. For Gospel communities, just as for persons, past events can be more present than present events, and likewise, future events can be experienced as if they are already happening. Christian hope depends upon this dynamic. However, this "memory" also implies that the experience of loss can remain a current experience even though loss occurred many years ago. Gospel communities do not always experience time chronologically, and keeping a balance between living in the past, being in the present, and living into the future is vital for the community as you lead them in doing the work of mourning.

ALL THE CHURCH'S LOSSES, ALL THE CHURCH'S GRIEFS

I borrowed the title for this chapter from Kenneth Mitchell and Herbert Anderson, whose book, *All Our Losses, All Our Griefs: Resources for Pastoral Care* (1983), addresses those normal emotions arising in response to a significant loss.[14] Although they wrote their book primarily with individuals in mind, their work is important for Gospel communities, too. *Have you ever thought that your community, even as it is expanding, might be "bewildered"?* And that this is a normal reaction to the change that occurs in a Gospel community when it grows rapidly, when new members and programs are constantly introduced?

Mitchell and Anderson identify six types of loss, thereby defining the multi-faceted nature of loss. The types of loss are: material loss, relational loss, intrapsychic loss, functional loss, role loss, and systemic loss. These losses represent the qualitative sense of loss individuals, families, and Gospel communities experience. For leaders of Gospel communities and for the congregations they serve, the ability to identify types of loss can function as a heuristic device to name and address the losses they experienced, are experiencing, or anticipate. In addition, the types of loss expose how vulnerable the body of Christ is to loss. It is impossible for the body of Christ, a body established through death and new life, not to experience loss! Of course, not all Gospel communities will be able to identify with all six types of loss, but every community will be able to identify with some of these losses.

Material loss

Did your church move from one building to another? Has your congregation ever burned down or did you ever have a building project?

How has your congregation's financial status changed over the years? Have you ever replaced one hymnal with another? These questions identify the first loss Mitchell and Anderson name: material loss. Material loss is the loss of a physical object or familiar surroundings to which one has an important attachment. You experienced the grief reaction against material loss if you are a leader in a community where the style of worship has changed, possibly to reflect a more contemporary style. Similarly, some elderly members of the community lament the loss of a specific translation of Scripture. St. Luke Lutheran Church, briefly introduced in the previous chapter, experienced material loss after having experienced financial strain following financial security. They, like other Gospel communities, minimized this loss out of fear of being seen as either too materialistic or too sentimental. However, such reasoning does not reckon with the fact that humans make powerful attachments with inanimate objects, and that loss has significant physical and emotional ramifications.

Some Gospel communities experience the loss of a church building, whether by accident, through arson, or due to natural disasters. Other communities close the doors of one church to move into a new building. A form of material loss seldom mourned but often grieved is the loss of familiar surroundings. A congregation once surrounded by farmland is now surrounded by housing developments and noise pollution. Another manifestation of material loss experienced too often by Gospel communities is the experience of churches closing their doors, some permanently. For example, in North Dakota alone, more than 400 churches founded by Norwegian, Swedish, Germanic, and Icelandic homesteaders closed their doors during the past four decades. Similar stories can be told about many areas of North America, especially about ministries that once served inner cities, where churches sometimes become theaters. As a poet said: "God is homeless, as every church becomes a theater or a gallery. . . ."

SEEKING RENEWAL FOR THE NEW BUILDING

Pastor Casey's church has experienced material loss. Pastor Casey serves a Gospel community named for the town in Iowa in which it is located. He says with great concern that his community is in need of "renewal and revitalization." In addition, he fears for his long-term presence at the church. That they seek "renewal," however, came as a surprise, for the church is a relatively new church. Eight years ago, his Gospel community, a ministry of an ethnic Protestant denomination, was located five miles out of town. A rural ministry for nearly eighty years, this Gospel community decided to move closer to town. To help finance the new church building, the decision was made to auction off everything. Pastor Casey reflects that antique dealers bought most of the church and that a lumberyard bought the wood. Some parts of the building, however, did fall into the hands of individuals and families that belonged to the church. The church bell, communion silverware, stained-glass windows, and other furnishings are prominently displayed in the homes of some church members. The only pieces of the old building incorporated into the new building were two stained-glass windows and the pulpit. In addition to the decision to dismantle and sell off the church building, the leaders of the Gospel community decided to change its name, for they wanted to be a "presence" in their new community and argued that their denominational connection might count against them.

Annually, the community makes a pilgrimage to the now-empty lot where the old church stood next to a cemetery. The "renewal and revitalization" Pastor Casey is seeking for his community is for them to reach out into their neighborhood. Eight years after moving into their new building they have yet to make an impact on their neighborhood, despite the vision that brought the congregation to town. Pastor Casey is wondering whether their inability to mobilize themselves and live in their neighborhood is related to the fact that the old church was never grieved because everyone had to be excited about the new building God gave the community.

Relationship loss

Were you surprised to read in the Introduction that mainline denominations lose between 0.5–1.0 percent of their membership each year? Thousands of congregations, possibly even yours, are affected. Relationship loss is a second type of loss. Mitchell and Anderson define relationship loss as the ending of opportunities to relate oneself to, talk with, share experiences with, settle issues with, fight with, and otherwise be in the emotional and/or physical presence of a particular person. Because of the pervasiveness of relationship loss, no Gospel community escapes this loss.

Middlebush Congregational Church has experienced rapid growth as they increased from 200 families to about 450 families over a three-year period. Recently, a few members of the community have told Pastor Sharon that they often "elope" to another Gospel community in town that meets in cell groups. They are doing this, they say, because in the cell groups everyone knows each other. They identify "care and intimacy" in this community, whereas they feel that the growth in Middlebush church has removed the caring and intimate nature of the community. Due to the rapid influx of new members, they feel they have not been able to connect to the new members, leaving them without a sense of belonging. Pastor Sharon is ashamed when she says that she feels guilty about not knowing all the new families. The growth and the added administrative demands it placed on her has robbed her of her practice to visit annually with every member or family.

Whereas Middlebush Congregational Church experiences relationship loss that comes with growth, Three Rivers Congregational Church is a community that knows relationship loss through a declining membership. Even families that have been members of the Gospel community for generations are no longer represented. In addition, Three Rivers Congregational Church has many elderly members; Pastor Beth feels as if she is doing a funeral every week.

A very different kind of relationship loss is acutely experienced when a church split occurs. Then the emotions of grief can be complicated by intense feelings of anger, resentment, betrayal, or even guilt. *How does one grieve relationship loss if you are still angry with the members who left and you see them worshiping in your neighborhood with the previous pastor?* Maybe you were thinking of leaving but decided to stay?

In addition, guilt feelings are often experienced when a member wishes a pastor away because of a disagreement and the pastor does leave, only to catapult the community into a crisis. Whether over personal divisions or doctrinal differences, church splits are often associated with intense conflict and disagreement and deny the membership the opportunity to process what happened and how they experience the split. The powerful emotions unleashed by a church split often override the need to mourn and to grieve.

Another poignant experience of relationship loss is the experience a congregation has when a person, maybe a member of the youth group or a beloved, long-time member, dies. A pastor, serving a community that experienced the death of a teenager while on a church-sponsored youth retreat, told me that he was blamed by the parents and by some members in the community for the death. A civil lawsuit was filed against him and the congregation. In their anger, some members of the Gospel community denied him the privilege to minister to them in their grief. Six months after the death occurred he decided to accept a call to another Gospel community. He expressed guilt over leaving the community when it was in need of pastoral care.

An unfortunate relationship loss occurs when a pastor betrays the trust of his congregation by engaging in an illicit sexual relationship. Often the same gregarious nature that makes a pastor a beloved person leads the pastor across ethical boundaries. A loved person becomes a perpetrator. This is an enormous loss for individuals as well as for the congregation. *Where will they find a place to say that they are angry, hurt, and confused?* How can their trust in the position, role, and function of a pastor be restored? Misconduct and malfeasance unleashes a painful grieving process of relationship and intrapsychic loss.

Intrapsychic loss

In addition to material loss and relationship loss, Gospel communities experience intrapsychic loss. Intrapsychic loss, according to Mitchell and Anderson, is the experience of losing an emotionally important image of oneself, losing the possibilities of "what might have been," the abandonment of plans for a particular future, and the dying of a dream. For congregations, intrapsychic loss is difficult to identify and grieve since it is often hidden and contained within the language used by the community to refer to itself.

Much of the loss James Dittes writes about can be placed within the context of intrapsychic loss. However, intrapsychic loss comes in many forms. Some pastors lament being "more like a CEO" and "less of a shepherd," struggling to live into a role for which they feel they are not gifted. These pastors have lost the image of themselves that sustained both their self-identity and their call to the ministry. Likewise, some churches refer to themselves using metaphors they gained decades ago. "The Steeple Church" would be such an example. The Gospel community has lost its "cathedral" identity and cannot answer the question: *Who are we as the body of Christ at this time in our specific context?* Rather, they spend much spiritual and relational energy to envision the community they want to be. Of course, knowing where you are heading is important to a Gospel community. Before a Gospel community can live into a new future, however, the body of Christ needs to know who it is and where it has been, or it risks the danger of repeating past mistakes.

Some Gospel communities experiencing intrapsychic loss are in danger of being deceived by images that no longer hold any truth or power. Other communities pride themselves in being hospitable, for example, yet no hospitality is extended to certain members, such as gays, lesbians, and transgendered, the elderly, or disenfranchised individuals and families in the neighborhood. Rather, young families with children or the promise of children receive all their attention. Also, some Gospel communities view themselves as missional churches, yet all missional responsibility is delegated to denominational missionaries supported financially by the communities. These Gospel communities do not know how to disciple people into becoming members of their communities. Another example might be those Gospel communities that see themselves as "a family church." Yet, as the community's demographics changed over the years the "family feel" got lost. Families are split apart as age-specific programs are introduced.

Ethnic Gospel communities, those congregations started by Dutch, German, Swedish, or other European settlers, experience intrapsychic loss in profound ways. A Lutheran ministry, for example, describes their community as "German." A demographic profile of the Gospel community, however, indicates that members of German descent make up less than 20 percent of the community's membership.

A Gospel community experiencing intrapsychic loss needs to discern whether the metaphors used to describe the community have the capacity to guide self-understanding and sustain the community. *Do these metaphors assist the community in the work of mourning they need to do, or does the fear of betraying the "father"—redefining their ethnic identity—hinder that process?*

Moreover, some forms of intrapsychic loss can be difficult to mourn especially if the loss was identified as a sin. How does a Gospel community mourn the sins of sexism, of racism, of homophobia, and of various forms of intrapsychic orientations if certain members in the community "benefited" from the abuse of power? How do you grieve an intrapsychic loss that has hurt others if the loss was "advantageous" to you? A conservative faith community in a traditional ethnic denomination had an all-male leadership. Women who served the community in influential ways wanted to be represented on the board of elders and deacons and asked their leaders to study sexism in the community. The study affirmed the women by naming sexism as a sinful presence in the community. However, three years after the study, no woman has been elected to the leadership yet, and no changes have been implemented.

Functional and role loss

Two closely related, yet distinct losses that cause grief are functional loss and role loss. For individuals, functional loss is the grief reaction that can be evoked when one loses some of one's muscular or neurological functions. It is often associated with the aging process and the loss of autonomy and mobility. Role loss, in contrast, is experienced when one's specific social role or one's accustomed place in a social network changes—for example, when retiring from one's job. In part, role loss is determined by the extent one's identity is tied to the role that was lost. Role loss is associated with a sense of being disoriented, a feeling that develops out of uncertainty. It implies suddenly finding oneself in a "one down position," a position that Mitchell and Anderson believe fuels the making of promises one has no intention of keeping. Wild River Church is experiencing such functional and role loss. The function the community played of bringing the wider society together every Memorial Day changed. They were no longer the hosts but were relegated to being participants. Likewise, Wild River's teenagers no longer need the community's function as the overseer of rites of passage such as the confirmation class.

A front-page article of a Sunday edition of *The New York Times* lamented the fact that churches are losing traditional roles and functions. In her article entitled "Beacons of Faith are Dimming on the Prairie," Patricia Leigh Brown writes somberly: "The flight of people from the North Dakota countryside has been silently devastating to this obscure but historically significant rural architectural heritage." She continues to lament the loss of prairie churches, which once functioned as "beacons of faith and optimism."[15]

If functional loss is associated with the loss of autonomy and decreased mobility, then the postmodern world as the paradigm that questions the validity of all universal truths (as metanarratives) brought about such loss for many Gospel communities.[16] Many communities remain uncertain how to proclaim the Good News in pluralistic societies or in a postmodern world. The role of being a bearer of Good News has changed. As such, one can argue that many Gospel communities have lost voice or their ability to speak.

Another example that congregations are losing their traditional way of referring to things (or of language) is their difficulty conversing with this generation of young persons. Many communities are silently grieving that they are no longer the overseers of rites of passage for their youth. New rites of passage, such as getting a tattoo, a driver's license, or receiving a body piercing, have replaced rites of passage once overseen by the church, such as confirmation or first communion. Someone told me recently about a community that sponsored an evening where tattoo artists created Christian symbols on human canvasses. Parents argued that getting tattoos in a safe setting and with parental blessing is better than getting tattoos in places that might be a health or safety risk. Some communities experience parachurch organizations such as Young Life, InterVarsity Christian Fellowship USA, Campus Crusade for Christ International, and others as threats, partly due to the fact that these organizations have taken over many of the roles and functions once played by churches.

Today's para-church organizations are very effective in reaching children, teens, and young adults with the Gospel of Christ.

~~Many Gospel communities remain a mere~~ token presence in Memorial Day, Independence Day, or Thanksgiving celebrations. Likewise, in a world in which the Internet has become a place where a sense of community can be experienced, where one can voice one's mind without any personal risk, and where one can find a database of knowledge, the church of Christ's role and function as a nurturer of community, as an agent of religious knowledge, and as a moral educator have diminished.

Leaders of expanding Gospel communities experience functional loss and role loss in specific ways as the community typically starts to function around small (cell) groups meeting in private homes. No longer can the leaders heal, guide, sustain, and reconcile the community as a whole, but their attention now focuses on empowering fellow brothers and sisters to be Christ incarnated to the members of the community. Hierarchical roles and functions are challenged as a broadening of the leadership base occurs. Still, people want the pastor, and not the elders, to visit during times of crisis. This is often experienced as a loss of power. Whereas previously a few persons "ran" the congregation, the gifts of many members are now used to care for and educate the community.

Systemic loss

A sixth and final loss Mitchell and Anderson identify is systemic loss. Systemic loss is the loss experienced when one realizes one is no longer part of the bigger (interactional) system. Elder Van Wyck of Voorhees Reformed Church expressed this loss for her community when she nostalgically stated that " . . . they built the mall down the road." Gospel communities historic to their local neighborhoods now find themselves marginalized within their societies. They have seen homogenous towns and cities grow into pluralistic, cosmopolitan neighborhoods and communities. Many of these congregations long for ways to reclaim a central position as they search for new ways in which to be a focal part of their communities. They remember when community events always included them and indeed often started in their building.

Physical and cultural marginalization of a congregation is just one example of systemic loss. Other forms of systemic loss can be: when a community changes its administrative model; when a pastor leaves or newly enters the system; when there is significant turnover in the leadership of a Gospel community; when members leave or join the community; or when a church split occurs. Of course, the Christian Church as a whole in North America is experiencing systemic loss. For this reason, it is impossible for an individual congregation not to experience some form of systemic loss as well. If some parts of the body of Christ are suffering, the rest of the body feels the pain with them.

These six types of loss can function as a mirror in which Gospel communities can identify the losses they have experienced. This is not an exhaustive list of the types of loss Gospel communities can experience. In my work as a consultant and coach to pastors and congregations, however, the six losses named here remain a common occurrence.

+ + +

MINDFUL DISCERNMENT

In light of the said losses, important questions to be asked by leaders and by their communities are:

1. What losses are we experiencing or have we experienced as a Gospel community?

2. How does the grief reaction manifest itself in our community?

3. How are we intentionally going to mourn these losses?

4. How are we living into a new identity after the loss?

+ + +

Processing these questions and the others to follow will facilitate the work of mourning your congregation needs to do.

John Bowlby, a psychologist who did significant study on the attachments we make and what happens to us when our connections are severed, can help us understand how the grief reaction manifests itself in a Gospel community by teaching us to recognize the symptoms of grief—the natural reaction to the experience of loss. The third volume in his "Attachment and Loss" trilogy, which is subtitled *Loss, Sadness, and Depression,* is especially important to the call we have to lead our Gospel communities in the task of mourning.[17]

IDENTIFYING A GRIEF REACTION IN YOUR GOSPEL COMMUNITY

Despite the fact that we were created by God to be in relationship, we underestimate the impact of loss on our beings and how long it takes to live through a loss. There is a tendency to suppose that a person can and should get over a loss not only fairly rapidly, but also completely. Bowlby states that grief typically has a long duration; that it is difficult to recover from loss; and that loss often has adverse consequences on our ways of being in the world. Although a grief reaction does not neatly progress through clearly defined phases, Bowlby did identify typical phases of grief, acknowledging also that a person does at times move back and forth between the different phases rather than progressing neatly. Important for understanding the impact of loss on Gospel communities, however, is not the phases per se, but the emotional, spiritual, cognitive, and relational reactions one can recognize within the phases.

From numbness to generalized hostility

The first phase of grief, the phase of numbing, usually lasts a short time, rarely longer than a week after the loss has occurred. This phase is often interrupted by outbursts of intense anger as a form of protest against the loss and an urgent effort to recover the loss. When you realize that the loss cannot be denied and is permanent, protest is followed by despair. Hope fades, and apathy and withdrawal set in. One typically experiences feelings of misery, sadness, and anger. Bowlby states that a child's persistent longing to be reunited with his mother is often suffused with intense, generalized hostility, directed at no figure in particular. Inherent to the hostility is an unconscious reproach against the lost person (whom one might have loved) as well as conscious and often unremitting self reproach. The result of such hostility is that the grieving person enters into shallow and detached relationships bereft of all intimacy.

The Sunday after Thanksgiving Pastor Robert announced to the community that he had given notice to the church board that his last Sunday will be the one after Christmas. He remains uncertain as to what he will be doing next, possibly pursuing an administrative career, but after "much discernment" he came to the decision that it would be best if he resigned by year's end. The speculations of conflict amongst the leadership were confirmed for the community. The month following his announcement flew by all too fast, with Christmas and year-end events taking center stage.

A few weeks after Pastor Robert left, his associate, Pastor LeRoy, preached a sermon in which he encouraged the Gospel community to become sensitive to how the Spirit of God was moving in the community. That very next day, Antoine, the leader-elder, walked into Pastor LeRoy's office to say that two members of the community were bringing heresy charges against him for what he said about the functioning of God's Spirit in their midst. Pastor LeRoy was blindsided by the news. Two members of the leadership made the vague accusations. Pastor LeRoy knew that they were hurt by Pastor Robert's departure and that he was not close to either of them. It did not take long for two camps to form, one supporting Pastor LeRoy and the other insisting that heresy had occurred. Many "camps" soon sprang up as the community was pushed into a state of generalized hostility. Some members began to question the way in which Pastor Robert left—he gave the community only a month's notice—blaming the community's leaders; others began to argue that the community is really a one-pastor congregation and that Pastor LeRoy is not a "senior pastor."

The leadership decided to contract with an interim minister to lead them until the new pastor arrived. However, it soon became clear that the congregation, partly because Pastor Robert did not process his ending with the community, was not doing the work of mourning. They were caught in the normal reaction to grief, but there was no intentionality to mourning Pastor Robert's leaving and to discerning the identity of the Gospel community in light of his departure because there was too much anger. Not knowing who they were in their history brought insecurity as they could not envision whom they might call to the community. An interim minister began to slow down the process of replacing Pastor Robert and began to ask painful and difficult questions aimed at helping the community discern a new self-identity.

Yearning and obscure goals

The phase of numbing is followed by a phase of yearning and searching for the lost figure. Yearning and searching often manifests in obscure forms and can be directed at an increasingly obscure goal with the disbelief that the loss experienced can be permanent. For a Gospel community, this phase of yearning to return to an original state can last for years. Sometimes, however, the searching manifests itself not in a way to go back into the past, but rather in how to redefine a bold new future. Gospel communities too often forget that a loss can never be replaced; it can only be mourned.

Growing congregations experience yearning and searching, too. New Hope Ministries developed out of Hope Church to be a true "megachurch," with a new church building that resembles a campus. They have a large staff serving the 900 families that form the ministry. Over the past seven years the Gospel community has had constant change as they continually built additions to accommodate all the members, as they added to their full-time staff, and as new programs were introduced. With so many new members and their attendant spiritual gifts, numerous new programs were started as ways to use these gifts to enrich the Gospel community. The rate of change and growth is so rapid that some of the staff has never been in the newer parts of the sprawling church building. They admit that the pace of change in the community is too fast and that they silently long for those years when they felt they managed well.

Recently, there has been a push by some members in the community to grow "exponentially." They admit that God has blessed New Hope Ministries significantly the past years, but that merely tripling in size is limiting God to doing only small miracles in the community. Rather, they believe that New Hope Ministries can be the fastest-growing ministry in the country, following well-known ministries that have been blessed as such. The staff, already feeling burdened by the current state of affairs, is anxious because the vision of how to grow exponentially remains vague. At a recent meeting of the elders, someone said that she wonders whether all this talk about growth is a way to shy away from talking about the difficulties the community is experiencing with its existing growth. She also asked why they have to grow exponentially since God has already blessed them. And what does this new vision say about God and about them? Tellingly, nobody followed up on her comments.

The spiritual and relational energies of New Hope Ministries are not only threatened by this obscure goal, but, as the woman pointed out, it can keep the conversation away from what the community really needs to talk about.

Disorganization and defensive exclusion

Avoiding conversation about what needs to be talked about is inherent to the third phase of mourning: the phase of disorganization and despair. Bowlby states that some of the disorganization that takes place as part of a grief reaction is due to the loss of one's identity and a dynamic he calls defensive exclusion.

The reaction of grief implies the loss of one's identity. For this reason, the work of mourning, which we defined as the intentional process of letting go and of living into a new identity, is so important. New Hope Ministries and Three Rivers Congregational Church have some sense of who they want to be, but they find it difficult to answer significant questions about being the body of Christ at this time and in this place.

+ + +

MINDFUL DISCERNMENT

1. Who are we as a Gospel community at this time?

2. How is our identity challenged and transformed by the constant change that has been occurring for numerous years?

3. If we find ourselves at a possible crossroad of sorts, what would that crossroad be?

4. Who are we without Pastor N?

5. What are the strengths and weaknesses of the identity we built with Pastor N?

6. How are we changing our identity with Pastor O?

+ + +

These questions of identity are difficult to discern. Somehow, Gospel communities have a much easier time saying who they want to be. Saying who they are, however, thereby describing the Context, the Culture, the Capital (or Resources), and the Conduct of the community, is easier said than done.[18] Describing the Context of a Gospel community includes historical, political, social, and other elements. Rituals, myths, customs, artifacts, the language the community uses, the hymnals being used, etc., describe the Culture of the Gospel community. The Capital of a community identifies all physical, financial, spiritual, or resources of persons and tradition of the congregation. Lastly, the Conduct of a Gospel community describes the ways of being in relationship of power relations; it identifies the leadership styles and more. In the next chapter these four frameworks of a congregation are revisited and a congregation's profile is given. When a congregation does not know who it is, natural ways of protecting the community are used. As stated, one such way is the dynamic of defensive exclusion.

In defensive exclusion, the Gospel community in grief excludes certain information from further processing. Of course, this is an unconscious attempt at protecting the community against the loss that occurred. As the information is excluded, the community guarantees that the work of mourning cannot continue. A Gospel community in grief can dwell insistently on details that are no longer applicable or facilitative of the grief reaction. Examples of selective exclusion in congregation are common. Conversations that need to take place, such as, "How do we mourn a loss?" or, "How have the losses we experienced changed our identity?" do not occur.

At St. Luke Lutheran Church's congregational meeting, briefly mentioned in the previous chapter, Pastor Gerhard opened the proceedings by stating that an audit of the community's finances found "that there are not enough sustainable units within the congregation to afford me or this church building." With his comment he reminded the community that they had experienced membership loss over numerous years and that they are at risk of losing him as a pastor. Closing the church's doors is also not out of the question. Suddenly, someone mentioned that the rent of a building the congregation leases to a small business had not been increased in years, and that the price of fuel oil has increased every winter. The person continued to propose that the rent be increased by $600 a month. For nearly an hour the pros and cons about increasing the rent and the amount of the increase were discussed. Some members felt that if the rent was raised too much, the small business might decide to terminate their lease, leaving the Gospel community with no extra income.

Finally, another person questioned whether the projected $7,200 of new income per year would in fact save them from losing their pastor and pay for building maintenance. The finance committee responded that $7,200 per year will not "save" the congregation. An uncanny silence settled over the community as this reality echoed through the room.

Degrees of reorganization

The numbing phase, followed by the phase of yearning and searching and the phase of disorganization is followed by Bowlby's last phase that describes degrees of reorganization. Bowlby's assertion that the degree of reorientation depends upon the level of connection (or attachment) between the person who experienced a loss and other individuals or between the group members who experienced the loss, is important to Gospel communities. In the work of mourning, it is crucial that all parts of the body of Christ participate.

In this last phase the symptoms that are part of a grief reaction will diminish or even disappear, but they might return during anniversary periods or when new stress enters the system. Pastor Robert's previous community will experience an anniversary each Thanksgiving, as if the body of Christ has an unconscious mind remembering the hurt it received. During these anniversaries, Pastor LeRoy can experience increased generalized hostility in the community as mild symptoms of grief reappear. Gospel communities always live with some memory of past losses and unsettling change influencing the way the congregation's members relate to each other, their neighborhood, and the world. Depending on the grief work they have done, this influence might be of a greater or lesser degree.

Of course, not all of the anger, hostility, or even defensive exclusion that one can find in a Gospel community can be ascribed to the dynamics of grief and loss. Anxiety caused by change might present similar symptoms. However, if you as a leader in your Gospel community can empower your community to do its work of mourning, you will diminish the anxiety within a grief reaction, thereby minimizing the impact of the symptoms on the community's life together. The symptoms, however, are signs of hope—they speak against the grief—and are not something that you as a leader have to get rid of as fast as possible.

GRIEF SYMPTOMS AS SIGNS OF HOPE

Symptoms of grief are signs of hope. When a Gospel community cries out against the pain of loss and change it is experiencing, it hopes that you will hear the hurt and the anger or see the emotional, physical, and financial withdrawal and the other symptoms of grief as hopeful invitations to initiate and facilitate the mourning process. The British psychoanalyst D. W. Winnicott wrote that the biggest mistake a community can make in response to symptoms that are destructive to all involved, is not to "see beyond" those behaviors or reactions.[19] Naming that the Gospel community is in grief and even identifying the losses the community is experiencing is the first step of the hopeful act of imaginatively "seeing beyond" the grief and envisioning a mourning process.

Hope in this context can be defined as a Gospel community's desire for a mourning process that allows letting go and living into a new identity. Grief has a compelling element, calling for the creation of a holding (or facilitative) environment. Creating a holding environment for mourning is your responsibility. Your congregation longs for (the possibility of) wholeness. Hope's close companions, however, are despair and distrust. If hope implies that leaders proactively initiate the mourning process in response to the identification of loss and the symptoms of grief, despair is when a grief reaction is not followed by the work of mourning.

As a leader of a Gospel community, you can invite despair and distrust in various ways: by not responding at all to the symptoms of grief, especially generalized hostility, thus being in denial; by letting the community know that they "should" be in a different emotional and spiritual place; by attempting to talk, coax, push, pull, or even preach the community into a different place; by being reactive to the symptoms, thereby acting without pastoral wisdom and discernment; and by using Scripture and prayer in manipulative ways. In addition, the symptoms of grief and the work of mourning can never be hopeful without significant conversation where the voice of every member in the body of Christ is heard.

Responding in ways that do not facilitate the work of mourning is a natural, but not fruitful, response of leadership. To walk towards the pain, rather than trying to run away from it is a courageous act that instills hope. Likewise, establishing a holding environment for the community implies remaining non-anxious; especially as changes that conjure fear and uncertainty are named and explored. A holding environment implies a safe setting that encourages significant conversation, where loss and change can be remembered without defensiveness or rationalization, and where these losses can be mourned and experienced. Such an environment, built though conversation, worshiping together, and participating in compassionate acts, is facilitative in nature, and invites a Gospel community to refind and live into a new identity.[20]

"Seeing beyond" the visible and instilling hope in a Gospel community requires that you as a leader in your community understand what happens spiritually and emotionally to a community that is in grief. To state it differently, what are the typical relational patterns within a "sad" Gospel community?

THE SEARCH FOR A DOMINANT OTHER

Your gospel community can experience sorrow or sadness. One way of seeing sorrow or grief is that it is the result of a difference that evolves between the way life is and the way it possibly could be. This is the insightful understanding of Silvano Arieti, who wrote on the "psychodynamics of sadness."[21] The examples of congregations that I gave in the first two chapters of this book can be restated as discrepancies between the way life is for a community and the way it possibly could be:

- "The way it is, is that the community is growing and expanding at a rapid pace. The way it could be, however, is that we need to be small enough so that everybody knows each other."
- "The way it is, is that our pastor left us under stressful situations. The way it should be is that we should have an installed pastor whom we love."
- "The way it is, is that we have been declining in membership for thirteen years. The way it could be is that we are a thriving community."
- "The way it is, is that there is distance and conflict between us. The way it should be is that we can love each other and dare to be transparent to one another."

The first element in understanding the dynamics of grief is that this discrepancy, between the way it is and the way it could or should be, takes hold. The second element is that a futile search to replace the lost person or object can cause the wish that a "powerful" or "dominant other"—a family member, a teacher, a counselor, a pastor, or even God—will reduce the gap that exists between "the way life is" and "the way it possibly could be." Individuals and groups who experience a loss enter into a bargaining relationship with a powerful other to miraculously change the situation. For Gospel communities, common powerful others are: God, a pastor or pastors, prominent leaders, or the leadership as a whole, or the latest church-growth bestseller or church-revitalization program. All of these agents are called upon to realize the way it could be. The work of mourning is thus left to the powerful other who must bring change without touching the individual lives or corporate life of the community. Gospel communities will resist functioning as the body of Christ, so that, in a quid pro quo fashion, the community can receive gratification and acceptance from the dominant other. Since the dominant other cannot do the work of mourning for a community, the symptoms of grief persist and deepen.

Arieti calls on caregivers to function as significant others, persons who can assist and empower the person who experienced the loss to return to some level of autonomous function and satisfaction. As long as caring relationships remain on the level of the "dominant other," sadness will prevail. For you as a leader in your community, being a significant other means that you help the body of Christ to identify and name the losses they have experienced, after which you facilitate the work of mourning for your Gospel community. You cannot do the work of mourning for the community, for such overfunctioning will deny the body of Christ its mourning, leaving the community in a desperate place. *How can you create the space in which the work of mourning can occur, even if you cannot "fix" your congregation?*

Dominant leaders thrive on questions posed by the community that communicate their helplessness, confusion, and uncertainty, for these leaders assume they hold all the answers. Significant leaders know that these questions are rhetorical and need not be answered immediately. Rather, wise leaders will explore with the community what it means to be lost. Certainly being a lost sheep is a common image in Scripture. Together they might discern the difference between the way it is and the way it could be.

Throughout this book, I envision you as a significant leader. Significant leaders help Gospel communities to explore the way it is, which for a community in grief implies having sober judgment about being the body of Christ (Rom. 12:3). If leaders become dominant, they will lead the community down a path where grief lingers into deeper sadness, hostility, paralysis, resistance to change, and apathy.

The grief reaction in a Gospel community can be diagrammed to show how significant leaders lessen the grief in a community, whereas dominant leadership actually causes more losses for a community:

+ + +

A GOSPEL COMMUNITY IN GRIEF

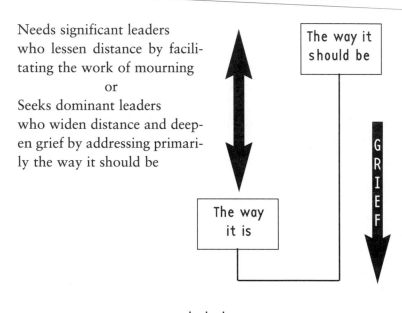

Needs significant leaders who lessen distance by facilitating the work of mourning

or

Seeks dominant leaders who widen distance and deepen grief by addressing primarily the way it should be

The way it should be

The way it is

GRIEF

+ + +

BEING ALONGSIDE GRIEF

Grief is the painful discrepancy between what is perceived as reality and what continues to be dreamed of as coming to reality. It calls for you as a leader to be present to both realities and with equal energy and integrity. Grief is not a disease that can be addressed by a "treatment model," where an authority figure pronounces a magic cure. Whether it is surrounding farmland that is slowly disappearing, or the community's youth who go off to college never to return, or a community that is growing by leaps and bounds, many Gospel communities experience pervasive grief and carry sadness.

You can respond to the grief in your community by seeing yourself as a companion to your congregation in its grief. Susan Roos, an author who writes about the companioning model, identifies the following elements of this model of caregiving and leadership: [22]

- Honoring the emotions people have (versus focusing on what they should think).
- Having curious creativity (versus communicating expertise).
- Learning from others (versus teaching others).
- Walking alongside (versus walking ahead).
- Discovering the gifts of sacred silence (versus filling silence with meaningless chatter).
- Bearing witness to the struggles of others (versus telling about personal experiences). And,
- Respecting disorder and confusion (versus seeking perfection).

For us as religious leaders, companioning takes us back to a well-established religious tradition. In the God of the Covenant, we have a God who is our true Companion. Wayne Oates, in his book *The Presence of God in Pastoral Counseling* (1986), reflects on the covenantal nature of God. He identifies God's "Over-againstness" and God's "Alongsideness" as paradoxical elements of the covenant. An encounter with the "Over-againstness" of God generates awe and reverence in a person.[23] The "Alongsideness" of God, on the other hand, is inherent to the covenant and emphasizes the relational character of God and the community between God, humanity, and creation. It receives its deepest meaning in the New Covenant and the gift of the Paraclete. God's "Alongsideness" brings intimacy, trust, fellowship, and collaborative effort to the God-human relationship. Although God enters into a relationship with humanity, God stays the Other in the relationship.

Gospel communities can rediscover the "Alongsideness" of God in their grief. By becoming Christ incarnate to the congregation, the community will experience God's face shining upon them (Num. 6:24). Such a presence, of course, is a near impossibility if leaders do not develop sensitivity to the presence of loss within the body of Christ, or when they believe that words or teaching can proclaim grief away. Some leaders might not know how to facilitate the work of mourning. Others have never felt the relief in coming alongside their congregations, always believing they have to lead. Grieving needs to occur from the inside out and church leaders can lead by example, becoming significant as they empower others to follow.

CONCLUSION

How do you identify the six types of loss Mitchell and Anderson name in your congregation? In this chapter I named six types of loss that are common to many Gospel communities. In addition, I portrayed images of how the grief reaction following these losses can manifest in congregations and how the body of Christ longs for a dominant leader to step forward to remove the experience of loss. In this chapter, therefore, I focused on grief as primarily an unconscious reaction in Gospel communities.

In the next three chapters I address how you as a leader can facilitate the work of mourning—the work of letting go and living into a redefined identity—in your your Gospel community by engaging in conversation, addressing loss in worship, and reaching out through compassionate ministries.

CHAPTER THREE

Conversation-as-the-work-of-mourning

Give sorrow words:
The grief that does not speak
Whispers the o'er-fraught heart,
and bids it break
> *William Shakespeare's* Macbeth

STEEPLES CRY. Congregations grieve. Your Gospel community has experienced or is experiencing significant losses brought about by various kinds of change. Like you, your congregation is paying the spiritual, emotional, and relational cost of loss and change. Ministry truly has become grief work. In the Introduction, I defined grief as the normal emotional, spiritual, physical, and relational reaction to the experience of loss and change. Mourning, in contrast, is the intentional process of letting go of relationships, dreams, visions, and more, of rediscovering and refinding a new identity after the experience of loss and change.

Gospel communities are called to do the work of mourning. Addressing the losses Western culture has experienced, Rowan Williams, the 104th Archbishop of Canterbury, says that "to recognize a cultural loss and a cultural crisis is (notoriously) not much a step to solving it; but it is something. It gives a perspective from which to question public policies and debates—even though the underlying issues are not easily able of being resolved by planning alone."[24] Faithful congregational leaders can do something: They are aware of the pervasiveness of loss and mourning within the church, they can help the community name and identify the losses that occurred, and they can facilitate the work of mourning that is needed. This recognition of what has happened, as Williams suggests, is the foundation for developing a perspective from which to question and move on.

The French philosopher Jacques Derrida summarizes the work of mourning, that process of refinding a new identity, as "to reckon, to recount, relate, or narrate, to consider, judge, or evaluate, even to estimate, enumerate, and calculate [the loss that occurred]."[25] Many congregations do the work of mourning unconsciously, nostalgically longing for previous times and places as they anxiously await an uncertain future. They might even ask for change, bringing in a leader for that purpose, but cannot live into that new vision for their community. Often, attempts to move away from loss determine not only the nature of relationships in the body of Christ, but they also drive the community's imagination. A congregation's vision and mission, and the difficult process of living into those self-statements, become the playground where unconscious grief roams. Whereas nostalgia takes one into the past, the work of mourning opens a future. When you invite the body of Christ to remember, everyone is given the opportunity to engage the work of mourning. Such remembering requires conversation. In your congregation, conversations—both formal and informal in nature—occur often. Conversation-as-the-work-of-mourning encourages intentional (or formal) conversation.

Elder Gabriel visited with a shut-in member of his congregation, Pauline, to inform her about the congregation's life and to offer pastoral care. As he gave her the week's bulletin, she noticed that the women's Bible study, which she attended for many years, was not announced. She asked Elder Gabriel about this "mistake." He affirmed the termination of the Bible study, saying that "they [referring to the younger women in the congregation] prefer to meet in someone's home and not at the church." Feeling left out and abandoned, Pauline displayed body language that communicated her disappointment and sadness. Noticing this, Elder Gabriel then started a conversation with the sentence: "Pauline, if I remember correctly, you were one of the initial members of this Bible study. Who were the other members, and how did this Bible study come about?"

Elder Gabriel engaged in the kind of ministry Doug Purnell encourages in his book, *Conversation as Ministry* (2003).[26] Purnell, an Australian pastoral theologian and artist, provides a new vision for ministry. By arguing for a conversational and thus highly relational approach to doing ministry, Purnell challenges how you and I do our ministry. He relies on the incarnational nature of conversation to facilitate change and bring healing. For him, pastoral conversation is always intentional, seeking imagination and hope, giving permission. Conversation avoids empty talk, clichés, and anxious silence. Ministry as conversation draws on the fact that conversation is the most prevalent conscious form of communication we engage in.

Recalling memories in conversation collapses time as the past becomes immediate and elsewhere becomes immanent. As Elder Gabriel invited Pauline to remember, she became a member of the Bible study group, remembering specific books they discussed and conversations they had. She belonged again. The intensity of such a conversation can lead one to be unfaithful to the past and to the losses that occurred. Pauline did not recall the times she did attend the Bible study, but because of personal circumstances or the dynamics in the group, she did not experience a sense of belonging. At times she had personal disagreements with another group member named Phyllis. From the vantage point of her couch, the Bible study was all good. Elder Gabriel noticed the idealization of the Bible study group but decided not to inquire about that at this moment. Derrida calls this dynamic, where remembering becomes selective or biased, "posthumous infidelity." Posthumous infidelity guards against seeing the past or the change that occurred as all good (idealized) or all bad (demonized).

The goal of this chapter is to empower you to facilitate conversation around the losses and changes that occurred in your Gospel community, thereby creating the space for your community as a whole to do the work of mourning. The chapter provides a partial answer to the question: "How do I facilitate the work of mourning in my congregation?" The condensed answer to this question is "By being engaged in life-giving conversations." I draw on the insights of narrative therapy and social scientists that rediscovered that life can be reauthored. As a leader of your Gospel community, I see you as being a narrative inquirer, soliciting and listening to stories of your congregation's past, present, and future. Narrative inquirers listen to those stories that are often told within a Gospel community and facilitate those stories that are seldom heard within the church. Leaders as narrative inquirers assist a community as it reckons and recounts, as it relates and narrates, and it considers, judges, and evaluates—all part of the process of finding a new identity. The congregation tells its future. Whereas this chapter envisions conversations in small groups and with individuals, the next chapter anticipates the specific conversation that takes place in a Sunday worship service. Conversation-as-the-work-of-mourning demands time and attentive, mindful listening. Such attention—or lack of it—is surely a measure of our commitment to individuals and how we create a caring community. Conversations like these seldom take place while you stand or when you keep your coat on, ready to leave and move on to the next conversation, person, or group.

A CONVERSATION ABOUT "THE OLD CHURCH"

In the late 1980s, a congregation in a small (but now expanding) Midwest town decided to relocate. They would move less than a mile from their historic building into the bigger building they needed, which would be conveniently located next to an interstate highway. Many members supported the move, but some wanted to stay in the church where their families had worshiped for generations. However, the new building was built and the move took place. Twenty years later I was called in to engage the leaders since the pastor felt there was little intimacy and a lot of generalized hostility in the community—especially amongst the leadership team. The pastor felt that the congregation resisted any change, whether in programs or in people. As I listened to the stories told about the congregation, reference was made to "The Old Church." It soon was evident that the story about "The Old Church" was a story seldom heard. Further inquiry revealed that "The Old Church" was handed over to the town's volunteer fire department to practice their fire-fighting skills. However, the firefighters could not save the church building. The members watched their beloved church building burn down. A colleague with whom I shared this story later tellingly suggested that there had been a cremation, but no funeral.

Some members, however, felt that the burning of the building was not a significant event, since there was a new building waiting. As the leaders told the story of The Old Church, it was as if the burning happened yesterday, still determining the future of the community as many members preferred to live in the past. Several conflicting stories were told by the leaders: stories of sadness and anger about the church building that burned down, stories of joy and gratitude about the new building (for which they already had a burning of the deed), stories of surprise and shock by new members that The Old Church was burned down, with feelings of betrayal that some members of the current congregational leadership were never told about this. There was no single truth in these stories: the members had to listen to one another, allowing each story to be heard.

The action of burning down a historic building has deeper meaning. Meaning was sought when someone stated that whoever gave the permission to burn down the church building must have done so to "get back at" those who did not support the move. Some of the long-time members, all of whom participated actively in the moving into a new building, strongly rejected such a notion, raising uncertainty as to what the meaning of the burning of the building was. Some members of the leadership team became defensive, since they or their families were involved in the construction of the new building. Other members of the leadership team were appalled that a building would be burned down, while others still were angry that they were never told that this happened. Furthermore, some members stated that the event had little relevance to where the community found itself today, while others interpreted the problems the congregation is experiencing through the lens of a burned building.

Holding all these different opinions in the narrative space is not an easy process. As the Gospel community's leaders struggled to gain meaning of this painful, yet very real part of the church's history, it was clear that context remained an important part of the congregation's experience.

After a few hours of listening to these stories, the leadership team stated that they felt closer to one another, saying that they never knew their sisters and brothers in Christ felt the way they did. A few persons mentioned that this was the first chance they had received to talk about this painful history of the community. Not everyone in the group shared the same understanding and vision of what the nature of the congregation is, and the community remains uncertain as to its presence next to the highway. The leaders, as they told the story of The Old Church, agreed that many years after the event there remains energy around its burning. They agreed that they would have to remain aware of this experience as they sought transformation for the congregation. The community's leaders created the space where the multiple meanings contained within the narratives could be encouraged and recognized. People could grieve the loss of The Old Church, and others could be witnesses of their grief. The leaders discovered that they were walking in the midst of numerous and varied stories!

Although it is difficult in itself to tell a story, the more important task is seeking the meaning of the stories. This allows for retelling, growth, and change. Of course this implies that you need to listen to stories that might be well known. In the telling and re-telling of stories, however, a reflexive relationship develops between living a story, telling a story, retelling a story, and reliving a story.

COMMITTING TO THE WORK OF MOURNING

Business consultant Peter Block, in his surprisingly pastoral book *The Answer to How is Yes* (2002), warns that asking *How?* can be symptomatic of a culture that worships pragmatism, efficiency, and consumerism (or commerce).[27] These powerful forces are neither life-giving nor spirit-granting. A leader who wants to try something truly imaginative needs to be committed to a process that fosters intimacy between persons and slows things down amidst a world that speeds ahead.

Block recommends that leaders should not avoid the How? question, but rather delay it until an appropriate moment. He identifies numerous questions leaders of institutions can ask as the How? question is delayed. These questions include: *What commitment are we willing to make? What is the price I am willing to pay?* and, *What is my contribution to the problem I am concerned about?* The purpose of Block's questions is to create space for new and exciting possibilities for individuals and for institutions. Block writes for the corporate culture, but his insights can be translated into guidance for the leaders of congregations.

Having identified diverse losses in your Gospel community, you as a leader and then the community-as-a-whole need to engage the following in conversation:

+ + +

Questions to delay or avoid	Answers to discern
How do we mourn losses or the pain caused by change?	Why do we want to address the dynamics of loss and grief in our congregation?
How long will the grieving process take, and how will we know we are done grieving?	What commitment(s) are we as the leaders of this church willing to make to facilitate the grief process?
How much will the grieving process cost?	What spiritual, relational, emotional, leadership, or other costs are we willing to pay as we grow towards transformation, healing, and a new identity?
How do we get people (young and old) to grieve?	What personal and ministry losses do we need to grieve as we lead this congregation?
How will we know we are grieving correctly?	At what crossroad do we find ourselves as leaders and as a community?
How are other congregations grieving successfully?	What kind of community do we want to create together as the leaders of this congregation?

+ + +

Questions of method are postponed for discerned choices. Anxiety around time (how long?) is replaced with concern about personal commitment. Questions are asked to discern the significant cost involved in grieving loss and change even as quantitative questions are received but not immediately addressed. Furthermore, leaders of a congregation create space for transformation by grieving their own lives and reauthoring their own selves. A shift in accountability occurs. Questions regarding the correctness of the approach are held back as questions regarding vision and mission are asked. Lastly, questions of comparison are avoided as you acknowledge the uniqueness of each Gospel community. As the discernment process above indicates, there is no cheap grace and no quick fix when one wants to do the work of mourning.

LEADERS IN GOSPEL COMMUNITIES INITIATE STORYTELLING

"The way it is" and "the way it should be" in a congregation expose the narrative existence of the body of Christ. Gospel communities tell stories—some often told and some seldom heard. To lessen the gap in any congregation that exists between the "is" and the "should be," church leaders can invite a retelling of the congregation's life and witness. Of course, inviting people to tell stories, especially stories of pain, is a challenging task. Theologian Kathleen O'Connor tells of her family, a family that describes many other families and most Gospel communities:

> My expressive, loving family practiced denial. It forbade anger, ignored sorrow, and created a culture of silence about hard things. From generation to generation, we practiced denial: we looked on the bright side, walked on the sunny side, and remembered that tomorrow is another day. Like many assimilating immigrant groups, deaths went ungrieved, anger lurked but could not speak, and broken dreams were barely noticed. Some of us lost great chunks of ourselves along the way.[28]

For Gospel communities, having a conversation about healing and transformation is difficult if the "chunk" that was lost is the ability to talk about such events. Like families do, congregations practice denial and hand down, from one generation of believers to the next, the inability to grieve deaths and notice broken dreams and abandoned vision statements.

Listening to stories requires a certain presence, since stories, being descriptions of experience, cannot be evaluated in terms of good or bad and/or right or wrong. Stories are multilayered and open-ended. However, narratives create tension that has to be contained by the leaders if the space for mourning, healing, and living into transformation is to be created. As Purnell reminded us, doing ministry is about having an intentional conversation!

Bringing out the meaning of an event breaks the culture of silence that often exists in communities. Suddenly individuals and the community-as-a-whole seek the meaning of change and transition.

LEADERS DRAW ON THE POWER OF NARRATIVES TO FORM AND TRANSFORM

The insights taught by narrative theorists and therapists such as Michael White and David Epston, Jill Freedman and Gene Combs, and by social scientists such as Jean Clandinin and Michael Connelly highlight not only the importance of narratives in the social construction of our realities, but also the facilitation of mourning-as-remembering through the retelling of stories.[29] Narrative therapy locates the emotional and relational (and we can add spiritual) health of people in stories that can be told, interpreted, and told anew. The narrative metaphor proposes that persons live their lives by stories; that these stories shape lives; and that they have real, not imagined, effects. Stories provide the structure of life. Michael White and David Epston write: "The narrative mode locates a person as a protagonist or participant in his/her world. This is a world of interpretative acts, a world in which every retelling of a story is a new telling, a world in which persons participate with others in the re-authoring and thus in shaping, of their lives and relationships."[30]

That narratives have the power to create change should be familiar news to Gospel communities who were not only founded on the Good News, but also find their meaning in communicating the Gospel.

Surely Jesus invited people to reauthor their lives! The question, however, remains whether Gospel communities can believe the good news that resides in the recalling of narratives of loss and grief?

"Narrative inquiry," coined by social scientists Clandinin and Connelly, describes research-oriented listening to and asking about experience. It initiates human agency, bringing forth improvisation and adaptation. Clandinin and Connelly write that improvisation, adaptation, and change are not only found with individuals who tell and re-tell their stories, but are also found with institutions. Institutions are driven by certain narratives that either motivate transformation or are "tension-producing devices" causing "interruptions."

Clandinin and Connelly refer to the work of Swiss social scientist Barbara Czarniawska, who links such narratives to themes of personnel management and communication in the workplace. Czarniawska calls her approach "ergonography"—an approach that uses narratives in institutions to foster changed relationships and intimacy between people. *When Steeples Cry* argues for ecclesiography, where the narratives of a congregation describe its spiritual and social construction and assist the community in doing the work of mourning.

As one listens to narratives, one needs to discern the different elements of the story: plot, character, scene, place, time, and point of view. These elements, if they are not kept separate, can cause confusion in the minds of the storytellers and listeners alike. Those telling the story may need assistance to communicate with clarity these different components of the story.

A narrative approach to ministry, which goes beyond a systemic understanding of the congregation, complements, supports, and empowers the vigorous and honest remembering-as-mourning. No longer can a community be seen as a system that resists change (through the systemic principle of homeostasis), but rather the congregation is a system telling stories that elicit change and transformation. As a leader of a congregation, you are a co-creator of the guiding narratives of the congregation, not an authority figure that needs to understand and change behavior. Since narratives encourage multiple viewpoints from many co-participants, leaders like you are freed from having the sole responsibility for the health of the community.

Listening to the body of Christ with its many members (Rom. 12) is important. It is no surprise that Dietrich Bonhoeffer, in his *Life Together,* names listening as the "first service" members of the body of Christ should offer each other. Bonhoeffer states, however, that "people are looking for an ear that will listen. They do not find it among Christians, for these Christians are talking where they should be listening."[31] When a congregation begins to tell stories about its existence, the possibility of finding a mutual identity is created, since the re-authoring and re-telling of stories are possible.

By placing the emphasis on stories that support lament and transformation, a congregation can grow beyond stories that communicate loss, grief, "stuckness," or problems. The multiple meanings of a community's narratives resist analyzing and evaluating the story being told. The act of recalling stories is formative in itself. Within stories often told and seldom heard, experiences are rediscovered and relived, and related to a new situation or to a changed future.

Narrative theory is clear that reciting a story is not enough, even if it is an important first step towards transformation. Rather, a culture—in this case, a church's culture—is changed when new stories are told (experienced or performed) and lived outside a counselor's office or a meeting room. The same warning would hold true to Gospel communities remembering their future. Merely recalling stories of loss, mourning, and transformation is not enough, even though it is an important first step. Additionally, in worship and in compassionate relationships, as the following chapters will indicate, the new narrative identity of your congregation can become lived experience.

As your community recalls different (and even opposing) stories of the same event, intimacy between the participants is fostered and the possibility for a new future is created. It is not uncommon for someone to say that she never knew that the other participants felt a certain way until they told their stories.

A LISTENING ATTITUDE

Conversation cannot occur if one individual cannot listen to another. Of course it becomes even more difficult when you need to listen to a group of people, where diverse voices want to be heard. Listening is a way of being with oneself and others. The listening attitude of a narrative inquirer opens space for new stories and new ways of being in relationship.

Your congregation needs such transformational space to be the body of Christ at this time and in this place. Within this space, leaders and community members can be asked how transformation influences the life of the congregation. The question can also be reversed; asking how being a the community influences the mourning process, for example. These questions communicate that the congregation, rather than being "a grieving church," is a congregation that grieves or mourns. Despite the fact that some Gospel communities do not experience healthy relational patterns, labeling a congregation a "dysfunctional church" does not facilitate a changed future where new ways of being in relationship are present.

A listening attitude facilitates the telling and retelling of stories as it guards against introducing a dominant narrative. You can gain a listening attitude by:

- Inquiring about stories that describe numerous experiences or realities.
- Placing the stories in a specific social context.
- Accepting the way that the stories are told—in word choice, the emotional content, body language, etc. Doug Purnell states that conversation implies valuing (not evaluating) someone's history, identity, future, wellness, illness, hope, despair; his relationships, faithfulness, doubt; her thinking, loving, hurting, worship; their meaning-making, and more.
- Inviting both the dominant and the marginalized voices in the congregation to tell their stories.
- Asking about the meaning of the stories told (and resisting evaluating the facts within the stories).
- Containing your own need to share your opinion, since your opinion can carry so much authority that it can stifle the conversation.

- Refusing to be the expert who can solve the problem, either by idealizing or demonizing the experience or person, or by bringing normative thinking to the experience.
- Risking or allowing painful or contentious stories to be heard.

The prophet Isaiah states that the Spirit of God empowers individuals like you to literally enflesh good news, to provide for those who grieve in Zion, to bestow on them a crown of beauty instead of ashes, the oil of gladness instead of mourning, and a garment of praise instead of a spirit of despair (Isa. 61:3). Without a listening attitude, this enfleshment cannot occur.

STORIES FACILITATING THE WORK OF MOURNING

With a listening attitude, you can initiate the telling of stories that will help your congregation do the work of mourning. This can be done by being mindful of the kind of stories you ask people to share. Let the following suggestions of different kinds of stories assist you as you focus especially on the work of mourning:

+ + +

Narrative inquirers ask	Nature of the narratives
What else is happening in our congregation? What do you pray about if you pray for our congregation?	Stories where loss, transformation, transitioning, and mourning do not seem to dominate.
Who is experiencing the new hymnal differently from the way we speak about it now?	Stories exploring different opinions and viewpoints regarding the loss or transformation.
What do you think Pastor N's departure under a cloud of conflict means for us as a congregation?	Stories about the meaning and impact of loss and transformation (consciousness) rather than stories

focusing on fact and action (who, what, when, where, and how).

Who do you think we will be as a community five years from now?	Stories about a future yet to be realized, where transformation and revitalization can be embraced, or stories with different time frames to extend the story beyond the present or the past.
Does this experience remind you of an earlier event in the life of the community? How did the congregation react as its membership numbers grew rapidly? How did the church grieve Pastor N's departure? How did the community react when the founding pastor left the community 20 years ago?	Stories describing the history of the congregation, its history with transformation and revitalization, its practice of mourning loss and change.
How would you describe our congregation's attitude towards all the new ministry programs that are being developed?	Stories describing the community's attitudes about and practice of loss, change, and mourning.
At this moment, how do you experience worship with the introduction of our praise band?	Stories about how the church is experienced now, rather than narratives seeking information.
How does the fact that we are grieving the lack of youth in our community influence the way we think about being the body of Christ?	Stories exploring the influence and effect of loss and mourning on the congregation.

That Christ is Lord is a primary belief we hold as a Gospel community. How can we draw on this belief as we are growing faster than we can manage our staff and programs?

Stories exploring the interrelationship between the values and beliefs the church has and its attitude and approach to loss and mourning.

Who can we tell about what is happening here at our congregation? How can we tell this story so that it has meaning for a stranger to our church?

Stories exploring with whom the newly unfolding stories will be shared.

+ + +

Posting the stories on newsprint as they are told, for example, can create much-needed distance between the person or persons who told the story and the narrative itself. Furthermore, it communicates that the stories are important enough to receive additional reflection. Seeking meaning promotes the living into a new reality and often does not end with a single interpretation or conclusion. Reflection (and not evaluation) invites mutual understanding so that unity in a group can exist; it indicates those stories that are not part of the dominant narrative or the issue under discussion. Also, such reflection helps leaders to notice beliefs, ideas, contexts, or dynamics that can impinge upon the work of mourning.

NARRATIVE INQUIRERS INTRODUCE AND CONTAIN TENSION

Clandinin and Connelly found that narrative inquirers, engaging organizations like churches in the manner described, cause certain tensions within the organization. There is the tension of temporality, since every story has a past, a present, and an implied future. The question, "Who do you think we will be as a congregation five years from now?" for example, implies that the way the past experience is reflected upon in the present is not the same as the event experienced for the first time, and that future reflection on the experience will be different, too. The question brings hope and anticipates the Spirit of God's active work in the life of the congregation.

Narratives also introduce tension around people. Every church member knows loss intimately, and it is important that individuals and groups receive the opportunity to narrate that process in their lives. Furthermore, no narrative is "people-free," and specific individuals and certain relationships will be named.

A third tension Clandinin and Connelly identify is around action. This tension implies that a story has deeper meaning that needs to be discerned. To assign meaning to the story, the deeper significance of the story has to be voiced. Since meaning is highly personal in nature, seeking action introduces a fourth tension: the tension around certainty. In listening to narratives, there is an element of uncertainty about the event's meaning, since different members of the community may interpret an event differently.

A final tension that Clandinin and Connelly identify is the tension around context. Context implies such notions as temporal context, spatial context, and the context of other people. Often these different notions of context are not shared by all involved, raising the tension between all participants.

Church leaders need to cultivate comfortableness with the inevitable tensions conversation brings. Containing your own and others' anxieties is a skill that can be gained. Containing the anxiety inherent to doing the work of mourning becomes easier if one has worked through one's own losses. I invite you to reread the case of "The Old Church." All of us who were present at the telling of the story of "The Old Church" experienced the tensions mentioned above. I could sense, for example, the uncertainty that set in as diverse emotions and different interpretations surfaced in the group. The ability to hold the tensions is a skill you need to gain. Your congregation will benefit greatly by your doing so.

NEGOTIATING CONVERSATION-AS-THE-WORK-OF-MOURNING

Besides holding the tensions within the narrative space, narrative inquirers have five specific tasks that facilitate the telling and retelling of narratives. The tasks are:

- Negotiate relationships.
- Negotiate purposes.
- Negotiate transitions.
- Negotiate ways to be helpful. And,
- Get a feel for the process.

A first and important task Clandinin and Connelly identify is to negotiate relationships, especially when people are at odds with one another or when the distinction between fact and fiction is muddled. Questions such as: "Did the events described actually happen? How do we know it happened that way?" may surface, but since no "objective" answer can be found in the narrative space and within people's experience, the tension has to be contained. Asking for additional stories by inviting more voices to remember, is important as relationships are negotiated. Second, you have to negotiate purposes by asking the persons narrating stories to explain themselves. Such explanation is work towards establishing relationships. Simple questions can further explanation: "Can you tell more about how all the new members that have been joining our congregation influence your experience of our community?" Or, "Your face shows much emotion. What is happening inside you as you tell this story?"

Third, church leaders have to negotiate transitions. The moments when narrative inquiry as a process is initiated or when the process ends are often contentious moments of high anxiety. Making room for people's anxiety, by informing the community of the difficult work they are doing or by urging them to remain mindful of their thoughts and actions as the conversation unfolds, for example, can ease the tensions. Fourth, you have to negotiate ways to be useful. One needs to work at remaining significant throughout the retelling of stories, especially at the beginning of the process. The participants in the conversation are uncertain as to what to expect, what to do, and what your role as leader is. A fifth and final task of leaders is getting a feel for it. This task refers to the fact that a narrative inquirer often feels isolated, pulled apart by the various stories, characters, and situations.

The first time you invite the telling of stories you might be nervous, but as you take this invitation to many groups of people, your level of comfort will increase. This level of comfort, in part, is brought about by the fact that church leaders become the keepers of the stories told. No other person or group of people will have access to the wide range of narratives told. You will act as the communal memory for a congregation.

Narrative theorists inform us of the importance in using narrative inquiry not only to understand institutions and individuals, but also to bring forth transformation and change. As you engage your Gospel community in this way, you facilitate the work of mourning. The stories told become good news, as the possibility for healing and transformation is created. A central paradox that church leaders have to contain is that congregations have to do the work of mourning, while doing this work is nothing more than being a community that can tell, listen to, and re-tell different stories.

In summation, the following statements can be made regarding the use of narratives in your congregation:

Narratives construct the reality of your congregation.

Narratives are always "peopled," as people live storied lives and storied landscapes.

Narratives imply movement between the personal and the social, between the past, the present, and the future, all within a specific place.

Narratives are not only complex and ambiguous, but they facilitate change and transformation. Leaders thus have to be open-minded and nonanxious as they anticipate the arrival of change.

Understanding the social construction of our realities is important in doing the work of mourning and remembering a future different from today. Since a Gospel community is a complex social entity, inviting stories that honor that complexity is important. In the remainder of the chapter, I will discuss how insights from those who study congregations can facilitate conversation as the work of mourning.

STORIES ABOUT YOUR CONGREGATION'S CONTEXT

How do you know that you are covering in conversation the broad range of transitions and loss a congregation experienced or is experiencing? The stories that are to be remembered in conversation need to represent the diverse life of the community. Nancy Ammerman, Jackson Carroll, Carl Dudley, and William McKinney in their book *Studying Congregations: A New Handbook* (1998), identify four frameworks that represent the multifaceted life of a congregation.[32] Each area can be the "location" where loss or transformation occurred and where mourning is taking place. Within each framework might even be a narrative that silently discourages or even overtly suppresses the mourning process. Likewise, a narrative can lead to the restoration and revitalization of the community.

The four frameworks Ammerman et al. provide can be summarized as follows:

+ + +

1. CONTEXT OF A CONGREGATION

- Congregational timeline (in relation to community, state, nation, world)
- Social demographics and forces
- Environmental (including environment in and around the church building)
- Political issues and power
- Economic
- Religious (affiliations with denomination or other churches, accountability, including relationships with other religions)
- Interaction of congregation and context or neighborhood

2. CULTURE OF A CONGREGATION

- "Ways of being together" that express the uniqueness of the congregation
- Artifacts (worship bulletins, newsletters, hymnal[s], liturgy, reports, mission statement)
- Myths
- Language used ("narthex," "potluck," "The Den," etc.)
- What the community does together: Rituals, customs, practices, symbols, habits, traditions

3. CAPITAL OF A CONGREGATION

- A congregation's "capital" for accomplishing its ministry and mission
- Capital statistics
- Physical assets
- Financial history
- Resources in people: gifts of people; relational strength; spiritual energies, etc.
- Reputations
- Faith tradition and religious heritage
- Equipped and competent leaders

4. CONDUCT OF A CONGREGATION

- "The underlying flow and dynamics of a community that knits together its common life and shapes its morale and climate"
- Emotional process of the church
- Leadership style
- Patterns of relationship
- Conflict resolution; problem solving
- Assumptions about authority; dynamics of power
- The process of mourning

+ + +

Since your congregation "lives" in these four "places," inquiring about the frameworks can be incorporated into informal conversations or more formal discernment. Various questions can guide you as you reflect on the four frameworks:

The context of your congregation

- What are the themes or issues that can be seen in our congregation's history (timeline)?
- What are our demographic data and how does that compare with the town's or city's data?
- What are the political, economic, and other forces that shaped our identity as a Gospel community?
- How is our congregation as a system with a specific location interacting with wider social systems (neighborhood, town or city, region, etc.)?

- How are we viewed by the other churches, people, businesses, and organizations around us?

Many Gospel communities who inquire in this manner find that there are significant changes in the demographics of their neighborhood or town and that they have become "islands" in their own setting. Some of the losses are not because of being left behind, of alienation, or even of financial insecurity. Rather, some congregations recall narratives of growth, of successfully negotiating the significant cultural shifts that have taken place in their contexts. Other congregations can recall stories of engaging their contexts in new and exciting ways, but as they were doing so, they had to change their identity. In addition, some congregations received a new context when they moved into new buildings or modernized their existing building.

The culture and identity of your congregation

- What are the complex network of traditions, symbols, and conventions that define the unique identity of our congregation?
- What are some of the cultural and social elements the members of our community share?
- What are the specific (age-related, economic, and other) subcultures of our congregation and how do they influence each other?
- What are specific artifacts (such as hymnals, stained-glass windows, furnishings, etc.) that communicate our identity?
- How have we created a "language" in our congregation to refer to certain places in our building, to certain groups or even to specific events that outsiders might not understand?
- How would we summarize the identity of our congregation?

When a Gospel community looks at its culture and identity, it often realizes that its culture has not remained the same. Rather significant changes can be identified even as a core identity stays the same. More important, some congregations find that the identity they thought they had and the identity they currently discern may not be the same identity.

The capital of your congregation

• What does an inventory of our community's spiritual, membership, financial, and other resources show . . .

• How are we good stewards with our building and other resources?

• How does the budget reflect our vision or mission?

• How can we draw upon the level of commitment within the community as a resource to facilitate not only the work of mourning but also living with transition, loss and change?

Generating narratives about the financial budget of the congregation will communicate, besides the financial resources of the congregation, the values and visions contained in a community. A story seldom told at a four-hundred-member suburban congregation was that the budget did not reflect the self-identity or vision of the congregation. This community, who saw themselves as a missional congregation, spent more money on education within the congregation than on funding local, national, or foreign mission projects. They confused education and missions. As the leaders discerned the meaning of this fact, they had to ask themselves whether they were good stewards of their resources, something they always had assumed. Another congregation discovered that they had a "financial relationship" with their membership. Much of the leaders's communication with the members was about the financial state of the congregation. The first page of their church bulletin, for example, was dedicated to the concerns of the finance committee. Never did they ask themselves the meaning behind a upper-middle class Gospel community experiencing financial difficulties. Conversations around the budget often indicate a relationship between finances and the conduct of the congregation. An inner-city congregation saw the financial commitment of its members increase with the welcoming of a new pastor who was called to the congregation after a comprehensive search process. Likewise, another Gospel community discovered that the tithing in the congregation decreased at the same time tensions between staff members became known in the congregation.

The conduct or process of your congregation

- How do the members of our congregation relate to each other, to God, and to the world?

- What issues are addressed formally (by the leadership or in committees), and what issues are addressed informally (parking lot conversations, Bible study groups, etc.)?

- Where does anxiety about finances, membership, or something else inhibit conversation-as-the-work-of-mourning?

- When does personal shame and anger or the inability to sustain a difficult conversation derail the process of discernment or even a meeting?

- What are the divisive issues in our congregation and how are relationships repaired?

As the leaders of Sunridge Park Community Church recalled narratives of the community, an elder stated that part of their story seldom told is that they shy away from conflict. According to him, not talking through significant conflict hinders growth within the congregation. Pastor Daniel, who typically chairs the board meetings, suddenly felt shamed, exposed, blamed, and incompetent as a chairperson. The pastor heard the elder as saying that the chairperson of the meeting was not effective in leading the church board and that his incompetence is the reason behind the avoidance of conflict. The pastor made a defensive comment and recalled examples of conversations that continued despite conflict. The elder did not respond, no one else followed up, and the conversation died down as a new narrative was offered. Trust was betrayed, a conspiracy of silence set in, and the process was stunted. The very dynamic the elder identified played out in their midst.

Recalling narratives that expose the conduct within a Gospel community inevitably introduces constructive tension to the leaders and in the life of the congregation. It often brings tension between the individual and the group; between stability and transformation, between the known and the unknown, and between remembering (giving voice) and forgetting (silence). If you as a leader can contain these tensions and not allow shame or another dynamic to derail the process, it will assist the process of mourning.

One congregation's "framework summary"

Conversation-as-the-work-of-mourning inevitably leads you to the questions raised within the frameworks identified here. One Gospel community that entered into significant conversation in search of transformation and a new identity drafted the following summary of their conversations:

+ + +

1. CONTEXT OF THE CONGREGATION

Social

- Marion County, Indianapolis, IN
- Population–197,800 (48.92% M/ 51.08% F)
- Median Age–30.4 years
- Fountain Square Historic District

Midwest

Economic

- Average household income –$45,557
- Per capita income–$19,363

Religious

- Whitewater Valley Presbytery
- PCUSA Interfaith Listening Project

2. CULTURE OF THE CONGREGATION

Rituals

- Singing—"Blessed be the tie that binds"

Values

- Excellence in preaching
- Music
- Christian education (especially children)

Traditions

- Children's Worship Festivals
- Gather Organ Concert Series
- Saturday Men's Breakfast
- Youth Mission Trips

Norms

- Lectionary preaching, church year

Artifacts

- Worship bulletins
- SonLight (weekly newsletter)
- Worship (hymnal)
- NRSV in pews and pulpit

3. CAPITAL OF THE CONGREGATION

Membership

	2001	1996
• Households	387	430
• Members	627	727

Budget

- Total income

    $798,977 $1,035,630

- Congregational purposes

    $723,130 $866,765

- Missional contributions

    $75,847 $168,865

Community connections

- Alive Ministry
- Alpha Course
- Witherspoon Street Ministry
- Louisville Presbyterian Seminary
- Finding Faith Center for Consultation and Counseling
- Church split 1970

4. CONDUCT OF THE CONGREGATION

Leadership style

- Autocratic (1962–1970)
- Shared-leadership (1971–Present)

Decision-making

- Centralized, hierarchical (1962–1970)
- Participatory (1971–Present)

Communication

- Worship bulletin
- SonLight
- E-mail
- Web site
- Program Brochures
- Kiosk

✛ ✛ ✛

As can be seen from this summary, this Gospel community is experiencing a decline in membership and that has had major implications for their budget. As typical for Gospel communities in transition, they have become inward focused, as missional contributions declined by more than 50 percent in five years. Imagine discerning the different frameworks of your congregation. Who might you, as a leader in your Gospel community, ask to join the exploratory conversations regarding context and capital, or conduct and culture? Some longtime members of your congregation, but also persons who joined your community recently can assist the discernment process greatly.

DOING YOUR PERSONAL WORK OF MOURNING

The work of mourning is doing faithful remembering. It is life-giving when a congregation says *Yes!* to conversation-as-the-work-of-mourning, even if remembering is a difficult task for a community. Churches tend to be the home of nostalgia, silently denying losses by longing for the past while rushing to an undefined future.

Facilitating conversation around the losses the congregation experienced is nearly impossible if you cannot converse about your own losses. Each leader has a narrative that is often told and a story that is seldom heard, and within these narratives, moments of loss and grief are present. These narratives need to be explored in a safe and confidential setting, such as with a mentor or a supervisor, a pastoral counselor or spiritual director, or a covenant (support) group. This kind of "inward" conversation and remembering complements the outward conversation about loss and transition that leaders invite in the congregation. As one can expect, this connection between the personal and the communal is often not consciously honored or examined. However, the relationship between grieving personal and communal losses can be facilitative of growth and healing for all involved.

A leadership team, in doing their work of mourning, initiated conversations around their personal stories often told and seldom heard. One member shared about his difficulty dealing with his prostate cancer. Another mentioned his struggles caring for a spouse with Alzheimer's disease. Yet another mentioned financial concerns and losing face in the community. A female elder spoke of a movie she liked and a deacon shared that he was adopted. Pastor Ivan shared that he is really excited about his family possibly buying their own home and moving out of the rectory. He remained silent about the pain and disappointment he carries because many of his expectations for ministry have not been reached.

Pastor Ivan has been at his congregation in a sprawling area for five years. His congregation's membership more than doubled under his leadership. His relationship with his son, however, has been a burden on his soul. He is alienated from his only child. His son lives a lifestyle of self-destruction and isolation, and father and son have a very conflictual relationship—one that mirrors the relationship Pastor Ivan had with his father. The abuse between the latter stopped when Pastor Ivan, then a teenager, broke two of his father's ribs in a heated argument. Pastor Ivan could never please his father, and that "blessing" was passed from father to son. New members to Pastor Ivan's congregation do not even know that he has a son.

Although the increase in membership implies that Pastor Ivan has much more work now and the Gospel community has more programs that need supervision and a pastoral presence, his salary and job description have not changed at all. He is filled with resentment—especially towards the congregation's board of elders, who have resisted the changes he wants to initiate, especially his desire to change the evening services and start group Bible studies instead. However, he cannot bring himself to initiate a conversation with the church board around his frustrations. Instead, his frustrations have become manifest in a passive-aggressive manner. For example, instead of spending time on sermon preparation, he plays solitaire on his computer.

At another congregation's leadership retreat, a female deacon stated hesitantly that she believes the congregation has lost its identity: that they truly do not know who they are as the people of God. A brief silence set in over all. Suddenly an elder interjected: "That is not true, we know exactly who we are!" The speed and intensity of his interjection did not break the silence. Nor did it challenge the statement the woman made. Rather, it spoke only of his uncomfortableness with not having a secure sense of who they are as a Gospel community. Other voices began to support the deacon, saying that the positive transitions of the past years left the community without a secure sense of identity.

When leaders are invited to share their own narratives of loss and mourning, or to partake in community conversation, some members will share a significant loss they are experiencing or have experienced, while others will recount experiences that do not open possibilities for healing and transformation. Yet in every congregation God places a few courageous individuals, willing to do their personal work of mourning. It only takes one member of the leadership team using the opportunity to move to a deeper level of sharing to empower others to follow.

As stated, sharing personal stories of loss and mourning amongst the leadership team builds community, strengthens the level of intimacy, and increases Christian care and concern. As such, church leaders model for the congregation the nature of Christian fellowship.

LISTEN TO YOUR GOSPEL COMMUNITY

After the leaders are empowered to listen carefully to the narratives contained amongst them, it is important that they reach out to the congregation as a whole and listen to the narratives that give shape to the community. This listening can occur formally or informally, but will draw on the insights and guidelines of narrative theory and inquiry discussed earlier in this chapter. Without the telling of stories, the work of mourning is not possible.

Some congregations announce various forum groups or even congregational meetings, where the congregation is led in remembering. Others study the minutes of meetings, listening for what was said and what was left out of the minutes. In some congregations, members of the leadership team visit Bible study groups, the men's group, the women's guild, the youth group, and other groups, asking all involved to tell their story of how they experience the Gospel community. Regular pastoral visitation is a great opportunity to inquire about how the individual or family is experiencing the congregation.

Whatever approach you decide upon, it is important that you give opportunities for the whole community to tell their stories of the congregation's life. Often, listening to the community implies that you must remain a nondefensive and nonanxious presence as narratives critical of the leaders or previous leaders are heard. In a congregation where significant change has occurred, the dynamics of loss will determine in great part how the congregation acts. If the congregation-as-a-whole is not invited and empowered to voice loss, they will hesitate to move into a new vision for the congregation.

If families are "houses of denial" as Kathleen O'Connor suggests, voicing stories of loss and mourning is "unnatural." People will have to be empowered to tell stories about the Gospel community's losses even in the face of their personal fears of embracing loss and mourning. A family who sees "tomorrow is a new day" is likely to resist the notion that the congregation is grieving.

CONTINUING BEYOND THE FIRST QUESTION

As you listen to the narratives that give shape to the life of your congregation, the questions posed earlier remain important. Those questions can assist you to begin to tell about a changed future. Follow up the statements made by members with questions that will facilitate further discernment:

- "I affirm your statement that we have many more programs now in the church compared to just five years ago. Maybe some of them are no longer doing what we envisioned they would do. What program or programs do you think we need to end?"

- "You would rather have us be a smaller community where we all can know each other. Now that we have grown in membership that may not be possible. How does it make you feel that not everyone knows you personally?"

- "We are no longer the community you joined. If we think of this as a loss to be grieved, how are you mourning this loss, and how are we as a community grieving?"

- "You are right. As a Gospel community we have not grown at the same rate as our town. What are the relational (or other) costs we are willing to pay to change that situation?"

- "As you were describing the way we as church leaders relate to the congregation, I wondered whether we as a congregation find ourselves at a crossroads of some sorts. How would you describe the different directions we could follow?"

- "I hear how you really grieve Pastor Phil leaving our congregation. He was your pastor for more than twenty-five years and he married your children. If he planted the seeds for our congregation to grow into a flourishing congregation, what kind of Gospel community do we together want to grow into?"

Every narrative, as it structures the reality within the congregation, has a specific meaning to be discerned. The search for meaning, however, is often lost when a story is evaluated. Passing judgment over a story of another person dissolves any listening attitude or the potential for change and transformation.

TELLING ABOUT THE FUTURE

Since narratives have temporality—a past, a present, and a future—it is important that remembering includes sharing visions of a changed future. Of course, working towards a vision statement will not be the first thing leaders do after initiating the telling of stories. Talking specifically about the future, however, becomes important as a Gospel community does the work of mourning. Envisioning the future, often by drafting or redrafting a vision statement, is a natural result of doing the work of mourning since conversation-as-the-work-of-mourning changes the identity of a congregation.

Regarding its vision statement, Holy Oak Community Church, an inner-city congregation, was thrown into significant turmoil and questioning when narratives surfaced that the current vision statement, now more than five years old, is nothing but empty words on paper. Although the congregation had a vision statement, they could not live into it in any significant way. Holy Oak had to grieve this intrapsychic loss and do so before they could begin the discernment process to draft a new vision statement. The persons closest to the drafting of the statement were affected the most by this loss. A vision statement is not merely a window dressing for the congregation, but persons have invested spiritually, emotionally, and relationally into drafting the statement.

The telling and retelling of stories itself implies that the self-understanding of a Gospel community, often communicated in a vision statement, will change. Central to the work of mourning is thus settling on a new identity that incorporates the loss or transition that has occurred.

LITTLE FOXES ARE SIGNS OF HOPE

Solomon, in his wisdom, stated that "little foxes" spoil a vine (Song of Sol. 2:15). Conversation-as-the-work-of-mourning often experiences the invasion of "little foxes" that spoil the process. When a person has not done his personal work of mourning, for example, it is very difficult for him to facilitate the work of mourning in the congregation he serves. Likewise, a person who is anxious about her personal finances might pour anxiety into a conversation about the Gospel community's financial situation. Sometimes a Gospel community cannot get past the generalized hostility unleashed by the grief process.

As a transformative process, inviting conversation on congregational life easily loses its impetus and focus. To some extent, the "little foxes" are signs of hope, for they would not show up if significant conversation were not taking place. Three primary dangers to the work of mourning through the telling and retelling of stories are: the danger of temporality, the danger of losing momentum, and the danger that comes from the mourning process not being ritualized (or enacted).

The danger of temporality refers to the fact that individual and congregational narratives come with a past, a present, and a future. Some leadership teams and congregations spend significantly more time on discerning the future than on the other two components of temporality. Such leaders deny, whether consciously or unconsciously, that losses have occurred and that the Gospel community is grieving. Instead, they tend to focus their attention on a new ministry or seek a new leader that should bring transformation to the congregation, often blaming the congregation for being resistant to the process of change when the new ministry is not embraced by all and when new realities do not materialize. In similar fashion, other congregations will dwell on the past, either with nostalgia or with bitterness, resentment, and anger. These congregations often have difficulty telling a future. By demonizing the present or by being pessimistic about the future, they are unable to celebrate with gratitude the here-and-now. In their mourning they remain stuck in the past. The psychodynamics of sadness, as described in the second chapter, can motivate nostalgia for the past or a fleeing into the future. Congregations that long for a nostalgic past or who desire to rush to the future often have not asked significant questions in any transformative journey such as: "*Who were we? Who are we? Who will we be?*"

Of course, rarely, if ever, will a Gospel community find itself in one of these two positions. A more likely scenario is that some members in the congregation will be nostalgic about the past, beckoning the congregation to go back to the "way it was," while others will urge the congregation with frustration to move forward. Still others will ask what the fuss is all about and some will already have done significant mourning. Differences of opinion and different ways of grieving are a given in Gospel communities. It is your responsibility to reach out in care and compassion to those individuals grieving personal and communal losses.

The second danger that can spoil conversation-as-the-work-of-mourning is the danger of losing momentum. Sometimes the process begins with a lot of energy, only to fizzle out and become stuck. Listening to your congregation is hard work! Like home improvement projects, it will probably take three times as long and "cost" three times more than initially reckoned. Still, conversations can end. Since grieving is a painful process, the telling and retelling a congregation does will encounter resistance, at least at certain times. Working through the resistance by acknowledging the pain involved is an inherent aspect of the work of mourning. When a transformational journey fails, the sense of failure becomes another intrapsychic loss the congregation has to grieve. What do leaders do when the process slows down to a point where no movement can be discerned?

The first question you as a leader in a Gospel community need to answer is: "Am I somehow stuck in my own grieving process?" When a leader experiences that the inter-connection between his or her personal stories and the stories in the congregation are too painful to bear, the leader might "discourage" the community from continuing with its process. Self-protection and self-perseverance will not allow you to empower the congregation you serve to go to places you as an individual are unwilling to go. Put in other words, we cannot grieve with and for the congregation if we cannot grieve for our own losses. Likewise, the leadership team, too, has to ask whether they continue to grieve the losses the congregation has experienced. If they cannot grieve for the Gospel community, they will not be able to lead the congregation to grieve. It is difficult, if not impossible, for a conversation to become derailed or stuck if the leaders keep doing the work of mourning. Leaders protect themselves against the shame they feel as narratives are recalled by entering into a state of denial, effectively prohibiting the work of mourning and the possibilities for transformation. Sometimes it is not shame that motivates such a move, but rather feeling threatened by the body of Christ claiming its authority. The fact that the members can lead congregations' ministries is frightening for those leaders who want to micromanage and be involved with everything in the life of the community.

In situations where an individual or a group is responsible for derailing the process, some form of guidance and accountability can help the process to get back on track. Ideally, a leadership team will have relationships and communication skills strong enough that they can challenge each other in this regard without pulling away or causing a total breakdown in communication. However, sometimes loyalties and the destructive use of power will almost assure that such challenge and support do not take place. An outside consultant, someone who can facilitate the conversation, can assist a process that has become stuck to get moving again. Similarly, one congregation can covenant with another Gospel community in town to be accountable to one another for particular tasks. The leadership team of the first congregation can initiate conversation the second community might be reluctant to ask, and vice versa. As would be true of an outside consultant interacting with the leaders of a congregation, the distance the other community has from the congregation that has to do the work of mourning makes it easier for the former to be a nonanxious— and therefore objective and helpful—presence.

The third danger in doing the work of mourning is that grieving stays at a level of mental awareness, never becoming an enacted reality, an effect. New realities have to be experienced. The next two chapters address how the work of mourning can be ritualized in worship and in compassionate companioning. In worship, the dynamics of religion and the movement of liturgy assist us in doing the work of mourning. By being in compassionate relationships, the possibility of mutual healing and revitalization is made possible. Whether it is through the compassionate outreach into the neighborhood around the church building or through living into the vision statement of the community, the process of mourning is incomplete if the new identity that comes out of the mourning process is not experienced by the members themselves, and more important, by others.

CONCLUSION

The work of mourning is to narrate, to recount, and to evaluate. Since the stories we tell and retell shape the day-to-day reality of a congregation, leaders need to be aware of the role of stories in doing the work of mourning. As narrative inquirers, leaders can invite both the telling of stories often heard and that of stories seldom told in a community. This work is crucial for congregations, for in one way, the work of mourning never ends.

Conversation-as-the-work-of-mourning does not end because change is a constant and conversation, by nature, is never ending. Doug Purnell correctly states that "conversations are always incomplete, ongoing and somehow interwoven with other experiences." Furthermore, the nature of loss and mourning assures that the work of mourning is never complete. "In the era of psychoanalysis," Jacques Derrida writes, "we all of course speak, and we can always go on speaking, about the "successful" work of mourning—or inversely, as if it were precisely the contrary, about the melancholia that would signal the failure of such work." Derrida places "successful" in quotation marks because he believes that the work of mourning is never something we can conquer with complete understanding.[33] Conversation-as-the-work-of-mourning can never be "completed" successfully. The only life that a Gospel community knows is one of transition, which implies the experience of loss. The loss will remain, the longing for the loved pastor who left, a past that disappeared, or a vision statement that failed, will stay. However, the ever-present nature of mourning need not dissuade you as a leader in your congregation from doing the work of mourning. Inherent to the work of mourning is the promise of new life, even if it is a life that will include mourning. For Gospel communities, grieving is life-giving and life-affirming. Conscious mourning has *dynamis* (power) that can bring forth new ways of being a Gospel community, or in the language of Derrida, "imaginable transfiguration."[34]

In this chapter I have sought "imaginable transfiguration" through the telling and retelling of a congregation's past, present, and future. Before leaders or a community ask "how-to" questions regarding its losses, they need to ask a series of questions that will lead to deeper understanding of who they are, who they were, and who they want to become. Asking these questions inevitably invites the Gospel community to tell stories about significant aspects of the congregation's life and to break the silence that often surrounds certain stories. As narrative inquirers, leaders can initiate story-telling in such a manner that it opens possibilities of a transformed future. The narratives of a congregation, whether they are often told or seldom heard, remain important to the work of mourning in congregations seeking healing and transformation after the experience of a loss or losses. Leaders of Gospel communities, therefore, have to assure that the narratives told represent the complex life of the congregation.

The chapter concluded by looking at three dangers to a narrative process helping communities grieve diverse losses.

In the next chapter I focus on how the work of mourning can be communally enacted in worship. Worship is the one place where the congregation consciously enters God's presence. It is a place of naming realities, of opening oneself to healing and transformation, and of being surprised by God. Lament, previously identified as a hidden resource for a Gospel community doing the work of mourning, I now revisit within the context of worship.

CHAPTER FOUR

Communion-as-the-work-of-mourning

Declare a holy fast; call a sacred assembly. Summon the elders and all who live in the land to the House of the Lord your God, and cry out to the Lord. (Joel 1:14)

GOSPEL COMMUNITY LIVES AN EMBODIED LIFE, a vulnerable existence. Your congregation knows confusion and uncertainty during times of loss and transition even as it seeks communion with its God and its members. Engaging in conversation-as-the-work-of-mourning naturally calls for your community to bring some of the conversations into God's presence during a worship service. Frederick Buechner once wrote:

> One wonders if there is anything more crucial for the preacher to do than to obey the sadness of our times by taking it into account without equivocation or subterfuge, by speaking out of our times and into our times not just what we ought to say about the Gospel, not just what it would appear to be in the interest of the Gospel for us to say, but what we have ourselves felt about it, experienced it. It is possible to think of the Gospel and our preaching of it as, above all and not matter what risk, a speaking of the way things are.[35]

Worship is a place where narratives become lived experience and where the work of mourning can take place. Pastor Kay knew that this All-Saints's celebration will be significant for her community. Her congregation has watched helplessly how Jonathan, a beloved member of the congregation, became stricken with an aggressive cancer that claimed his life two weeks ago. His family's and her parishioners's grief is still raw barely a week after the funeral. They had numerous healing services for Jonathan and anointed him with oil days before his death. Some prayed for and believed a miracle would occur. Others just prayed that Jonathan would become a sign of God's reign. Jonathan's death unleashed significant questioning about God, the power of prayer, and living in a broken reality. Pastor Kay hears how the congregation is questioning God and life during her regular visitation and house calls. Even before the service started, tears started to flow when Jonathan's wife, Ruth, and their daughter walked down the aisle to take their regular seats. There was a silent acknowledgment that today's lighting of candles for those who died the past two years will be doing the work of mourning.

The work of mourning is the intentional process of letting go of relationships, dreams, visions, and more, of rediscovering and refinding a new identity after the experience of loss and change. As a congregation gathers in communion and worship, a space is created where God's Spirit brings hope, and where it heals and revitalizes. Similarities between the spiritual, emotional, and relational dynamics of a worship service and an intentional process of moving beyond grief abound. Worship and the process of mourning transform identity, unlock vision, and invite one to flourish despite the circumstances. Both invite confession of one's absolute dependence on God as the Good News and other stories are told and retold. Worship and mourning imply that some working through will occur, that within the moments of remembering, some refinding of a new identity will occur.[36] Whether in worship or in mourning, one enters the invisible communion of others who also grieve and are longing for the affirmation of a new life or future. In addition, within both processes the unspeakable is voiced with particularity, amnesia is annihilated, and hope is fostered that drives silent despair away. Last of all, worship and mourning either facilitates a sense of community or communion, breaking isolation and alienation, or it divides the community.

This chapter describes how a worship experience can create the space for the work of mourning to occur. Ironically, changes in how a Gospel community worships is one of the causes of the dynamics of loss and grief in many congregations. Still, the elements within a worship service, approaching God, the sermon, singing, offering prayers, and partaking in baptism or the Lord's Supper, to name a few, have a dynamic rhythm that invites the community to refind a new identity and to expose its soul to God. The communal mourning we find in a book such as the Book of Lamentations or in the Psalms of Lament provides us with a language of pain, fear, and uncertainty, but also of hope and a new future, the very language the work of mourning requires and encourages. Communion-as-the-work-of-mourning is joining those voices that reclaim lament as a resource in a culture of praise choruses, worship wars, and congregational instability.

+ + +

MINDFUL DISCERNMENT

Communion-as-the-work-of-mourning highlights the importance of worship:

- How does the way our congregation communes with God in worship transform identities, whether individual or corporate?

- How does our Gospel community invite the expression of absolute dependence upon God, whether through the confession of sins, through prayers, or through music?

- What stories of Scripture do you often recall to dialogue with the stories of your congregation?

- Describe the hope that is fostered for the community as you worship together.

- As you worship, are the members of our congregation active participants, invisible listeners, or anonymous visitors?

- How do you facilitate the work of mourning through your sermons and through leading a community in worship?

+ + +

THE PSYCHODYNAMICS OF LIFE AND WORSHIP

What happens to one's being during a worship service? And how does that relate to the way we live the rest of the week? Imagine a parishioner. Ryan went out to breakfast and read a newspaper before coming to worship. His mind is still on the war he read about when he enters the sanctuary. The playing of the organ quiets Ryan's mind and prepares him for what is to come. He slowly lets go of the thoughts of war. The liturgist welcomes all to the service and announces a hymn that proclaims God's faithfulness through the ages. Shortly after that, Ryan is invited to confess his sins before God, and he states in unison that he is totally depraved and in need of God's redemption. This is followed by a sermon that focuses on the presence of domestic violence in our families. Ryan remembers the hard hands of his father as he is held by the pastor's words. The sermon is followed by Ryan handing over his offering. He sings again and receives a blessing from the pastor. He leaves the sanctuary to read the finance section of his newspaper at home, drinking his favorite herbal tea.

Ryan moved from an independent position in worldly life, to expressing dependence on God in worship, back to an independent position. This kind of movement intrigues Bruce Reed, a British practical theologian and sociologist of religion. Reed is interested in the similarities between the lives we live Monday through Saturday and the experience we have on Sunday when we enter a worship service.[37] Reed, who draws on the work of D.W. Winnicott, argues that we oscillate between periods of relative independence and moments of expressing absolute dependence. He uses the term "relative independence" since it is impossible for us to be absolutely independent.

A movement of oscillation is distinguished from a cyclical movement in that Reed envisions an oscillation not to be repetitive, with each beginning and ending within the oscillation movement different since the movement facilitates transformation. Reed assumes that a person such as Ryan left the worship service in a different state even though he returned to read the financial section of his newspaper. You can imagine numerous oscillation movements as a winding spiral, where no beginning is the same as the previous ending.

During moments of absolute dependence, Reed states that individuals and communities experience a state of "in-needness" that compels us to reach out to God and others as a source of healing, bringing us into relationship. "In-needness" has a relational quality and should be distinguished from having needs. The former is a given state regardless of the physiological, emotional, or material needs that we carry. When we experience "in-needness," we need something to hold us. Reed identifies the worship service as an experience that can hold persons when they are in a position of absolute dependence. Ryan arrived at the worship service distressed about what he read in his newspaper. The service, however, created the space for Ryan not only to express his absolute dependence upon God, which removed some of his anxiety about war, but also to revisit his painful childhood. His fear now, the same fear he knew as a child, was named and honored before God.

For Reed, the oscillation between relative independence and dependence is not only a metaphor for life, but indicates the essential conditions describing the well-being of Christian community. As a person oscillates between relative independence and absolute dependence, moments that require healing and transformation are revisited. We, as the congregation, can revisit those "frozen moments" of our lives. "Frozen moments" are those experiences that require a lot of spiritual and emotional energy to keep the pain away from our consciousness. In worship, we can allow a "frozen moment" to be "thawed" in a safe holding environment. In worship today, Ryan could "thaw" the painful memories of childhood and release some of the fears he has been carrying since then.

The transformation process and the refinding that takes place during the oscillation movement are brought about by the introduction of symbolic material during the stage of absolute dependence. Through the preaching of the Word of God or other ritual elements in worship, symbolic contact occurs. For a Gospel community, the symbolic material invites the community to be the body of Christ in the world. By preaching on domestic violence and how we can lose our childhoods, Ryan's pastor created the space for him to revisit his painful childhood in the safe presence of God. He heard that it was his father's responsibility as a parent and an adult to create a safe place for Ryan's family. This relieved Ryan of the sense of responsibility he always felt, that he, as a nine year old, had to protect himself and his family against his father's drunken rages and failed. When the pastor gave the final blessing, Ryan felt a strange peace even though a flood of emotion came to him as he remembered his childhood. It felt as if God did turn God's face towards him, as the blessing said.

Although Bruce Reed writes about individuals engaging life and worship, his oscillation theory can be informative for Gospel communities as they live into their call of being the body of Christ in their specific contexts. Worship begins with individuals forming a visible community to leave again as individuals. This happens in a fourfold oscillation process: Realization, regression to dependence, identification, and transformation to the next stage of realization.[38]

The first stage, called *realization,* describes a community as it lives in reality. This is Ryan reading his newspaper before coming to church. He follows the news about the wars around the world with silent anxiety. It is safe to assume that most members of your Gospel community are in the stage of realization when they enter worship Sunday morning. Realization is determined by the Gospel community's inward experience. If the community experienced or is experiencing significant loss and transition, the dynamics of loss and grief will determine the inward experience of the community. It is the inward experience of a community that determines the way the community will engage its outward contexts.

The second stage is called *regression to dependence* and symbolizes the inward withdrawal by the Gospel community from being the body of Christ in its context. Here Ryan is being invited to take his mind off of the newspaper and to worship God. With the community, Ryan professes his dependence upon God. Your church members step out of the world they inhabit the rest of the week and step into the presence of God. Ironically, Reed states that when one enters into the stage, one's ability to work with other individuals diminishes, since absolute dependence reminds the members of the Gospel community and the community itself of its isolation, vulnerability, and mortality.

The third stage is called *identification* as the community searches for a Dependent Object with whom to identify to be a container for their anxieties, hopes, and joys. The Object assists the community to feel secure and "real." Here, a preacher and the community rely on the symbols, visions, rituals, and narratives of Scripture that can "thaw" frozen moments—those painful experiences in the life of the Gospel community. This thawing process is complemented by a process of identification that refinds a communal identity. Within the stage of identification, Ryan was taken back to his family of origin, which was an abusive, alcoholic system. He is shown a vision of family members loving each other, caring deeply for each other, and watching each other thrive. As Ryan revisits his past, painful memories come to mind, such as the one time when he wanted to protect his mother, and his father's fist knocked out his two front teeth.

The fourth and last stage of the oscillation movement is called *transformation to realization* and anticipates the next realization stage. Ryan made a silent vow to speak out against physical abuse as often as he can. He promised himself that he will not be fear-driven— a way of being he learned in childhood. Maybe he'll become a Big Brother to someone? The redemptive transformation suggests that Ryan and the community have progressed on the road of becoming the body of Christ, moving from symbolic activity to being the hands and feet of Christ in the world. For a Gospel community, its newly informed identity can now be expressed outwardly, for example, by engaging in compassionate and caring relationships.

+ + +

MINDFUL DISCERNMENT

As you think about your community and worship, questions that can lead you through the oscillation process are:

- What is our Gospel community's inward experience? How do we voice the ways we relate to ourselves, the world, and God in worship? How does my focus on the community's needs and the needs of the wider society transcend the radical individualism of our culture?

- How do we as leaders of our community help our community to move towards a position of absolute dependence upon God? How can we express our absolute dependence upon God in confession of sin, prayers, sermons, and hymns or other music?

- What are the primary symbols, rituals, and narratives that are being communicated to our community? How are the painful and joyous moments in the life of the congregation voiced in the worship service? What identity is honored and being envisioned by my sermon and through the worship service?

- What ministries of education, service, and care are empowered and supported through the worship service? How do we live differently because of the sermon and the experience of worship we had? How does the naming of the community's losses in the presence of God empower the community to embrace the work of mourning? How are people encouraged not to become reactive or resistant to change? What is our Gospel community's inward experience? How do we voice the ways we relate to ourselves, the world, and God in worship?

+ + +

Within worship, then, one finds an oscillation process that facilitates the work of mourning for individuals and for your congregation. The way you voice the loss and transitions that the community experienced is therefore central to communion-as-the-work-of-mourning. Because preaching the Word of God is a central moment in most worship services, it is addressed next. The sermon can create the space for reexperiencing loss and transition, even as that experience is voiced before God. This space is created by voicing the confusion and fear change brings in the form of a lament.

REMEMBERING, TRUTH-TELLING, AND MOURNING IN THE BOOK OF LAMENTATIONS

How deserted lies the city, once so full of people!
How like a widow is she, who once was great among the nations!

> She who was queen among the provinces has now become a slave.
> The roads to Zion mourn, for no one comes to her appointed feasts.
> All her gateways are desolate, her priests groan,
> her maidens grieve, and she is in bitter anguish. (Lam. 1:1, 4)

You have covered yourself with a cloud so that no prayer can get through. (Lam. 3:44)

> Remember, O LORD, what has happened to us; look, and see our disgrace. Our inheritance has been turned over to aliens, our homes to foreigners. We have become orphans and fatherless, our mothers like widows. (Lam. 5:1–3)

The Book of Lamentations is a summons to companionship. For this reason it can inform your worship. In the previous chapter, Kathleen O'Connor shared with us the story of her family who "created a culture of silence about hard things." In her book, *Lamentations and the tears of the world* (2002), she writes that

> Lamentations deserves a more prominent place in the liturgical life of believing Christian communities than it presently holds.... Its potent language and affecting forms, as well as its capacities to house sorrow and teach resistance, can assist us in coping with present despair and future grief.[39]

Lamentations becomes a mirroring witness to a community that lives with untold grief, fear, and doubt.

Despite the fact that the book is an elaborated lament, it is not a depressing book. It does not cause sorrow, hostility, or despair, for it cannot evoke feelings a person does not already know. Rather, it brings hope as it reveals sadness and fear. O'Connor further states that without the Book of Lamentations, we would lose a resource for personal, familial, and communal crises, and we cannot connect to other peoples. "Compassion-as-the-work-of-mourning," the title of the next and final chapter, follows O'Connor when she says that the ability to mourn opens our eyes to the suffering that is in the world.

As Jacques Derrida warned us, remembering is the essence of grieving and needs to be done with "posthumous fidelity." The Book of Lamentations is unrivaled in its faithful communal witnessing to the pain of loss in the life of Israel. Gospel communities can gain much courage from the witness of Lamentations, for "the Book of Lamentations is about the collapse of a physical, emotional, and spiritual universe of an entire people, not about individual sorrows except in a metaphoric and symbolic manner."[40]

The poetry of Lamentations arose in the aftermath of a catastrophic historical event, the destruction of Jerusalem, although it remains uncertain which of the many invasions of Jerusalem prompted the lament. The book honors voices of loss, pain, and despair, and in doing so breaks the isolation of a grieving community. For Gospel communities, the people of Israel are role models in giving voice to loss and suffering. Lamentations gives voice to communal losses, disappointments, and the expression of hope and new beginnings. The book is a shelter of sorrow where our humanity can be restored to discover compassion, and where the body of Christ can find revitalization.

O'Connor refers to the work of Arthur Frank, who explores the dynamics of terminal illness. Frank often finds individuals suffering a terminal illness in "narrative wreckage," by which he means lives where all possibilities disappeared, where despair rules.[41] No doubt you experienced some degree of "narrative wreckage" when you became a narrative inquirer and listened to the stories of your community. Lamentations facilitate narrative restoration. Its emphasis on truth-telling brings hope as silences—even the silences caused by misunderstandings of the Christian faith that dissuade grieving and mourning—are broken.

If your Gospel community is one of disorientation seeking reorientation, the prayers of Lamentations can assist your community to verbalize its sorrow and uncertainty as your community awaits a new future.[42] Lamentations 1:1 sets a clear agenda (O'Connor's translation):

How lonely sits the city once great with people!
She has become like a widow, she who once was great among the nations.
A princess among the provinces, she is now in forced labor.

And verse 11:

All the people are groaning, seeking bread.
They give their precious things for food and to stay alive.
YHWH, look and pay attention for I have become worthless!

The truth-telling of Lamentations seeks God's presence by verbalizing the "way it is" and the "way it should be" (which we addressed in Chapter 2). It voices the cacophony of emotions a community experiences in a dirge, a funeral song proclaiming a death and a summoning of the community to grieve. When a steeple cries, the community needs to be summoned to mourn the diverse losses experienced over many years or they are at risk of remaining in grief. Like a Jeremiah of old, who mourned the sinful nature of his people, church leaders and the community need to mourn "the way it is" in their congregation.

Whether your Gospel community identifies with Lamentations's lament against isolation and loneliness (Lam. 1:1), her mourning for people not coming to the feast (Lam. 1:4), her lamenting the destructive rage of God (Lam. 1:16), or the physical destruction of the city (Lam. 2:7–9), the people of God can find solace and empowerment in the memory of Israel crying out to God in her grief. The grief of Israel is pervasive, vivid, and palpable. It was a living force permeating the city so thoroughly that even inanimate objects, such as roads, walls, and gates, were grieving.

Can you envision bringing the unspeakable to be heard? Imagine voicing the lament that some of your members carry even as others are rejoicing that change is occurring? The Book of Lamentations can empower you and your community to "bring the unspeakable to expression." Of course, in conversation-as-the-work-of-mourning your community voices the impact of loss and change. Voicing our deepest pain, insecurity, and joys in God's presence and within the dynamics of worship invites the comforting Spirit of God to bring healing and restoration. In Lamentations, no voice wins out, unifies, or dominates the claims of other voices. You have the voices lamenting the loss of the city even as you have the voice of the strongman expressing hope (Lam. 3:21ff).

I was invited to offer guidance to a large congregation who were processing the departure of their two senior pastors after painful experiences. One of the pastors took a few families with him as he started a new Gospel community almost within eyesight of his previous congregation. The diversity of voices was anxiety producing: Some were deeply hurt by the pastors's conduct; some were angry with one pastor—not always the same one; some were saddened by the families who left; others blamed their leaders for not doing anything when the conflict became known; and still others said that this was a great opportunity to re-envision the community. After the consultation, many expressed their gratitude towards me for slowing down the process and for giving them permission to mourn what has happened in their community. They felt relieved and hopeful. But some reached out to me in anger and confusion. These members suggested that I was overlooking the sin of some members by not requesting "them" to confess the sins "they" committed in this regard. As a leader of a Gospel community, you need not fear the diversity of voices nor be reactive to the sorrow and confusion that seeks an uncomplicated explanation or unity.

Telling the story of loss or growth and transition is crucial for Gospel communities to move beyond the position of grief. O'Connor writes that when a people's symbolic narrative collapses, they cannot move toward the future. Such people are without a plan or a rudder; they have nothing to guide their steps, no incentive to claim their identity, nothing to provide a sense of safety. In the Book of Lamentations, narrative collapse (or wreckage) is a real danger because the voice of God is elusive throughout the Book, but without God, the people of Jerusalem have no story, no future. Where will they find new life? This primal fear motivates a plea for God to appear (Lam. 1:11, 20). The Book of Lamentations witnesses to a shattered group with a future yet to be revealed. It presents suffering in all its rawness. O'Connor writes:

> Because of God's missing voice, Lamentations honors truth-telling and denies "denial." Human speech about suffering matters so much that Lamentations presents it in all its rawness. It lingers over pain and gives words to mute suffering. A house for sorrow and a school for compassion, Lamentations teaches resistance, it liberates passions, and gives us prayers for the world's tears. These may be enormous claims for so small a book. Yet honoring the voices of suffering, the book undermines familial and cultural systems that deny it.[43]

The Book of Lamentations breaks the silence around living with unbearable emotions and unacceptable impulses—the very building blocks of trauma. The church, grieving for decades, has been traumatized. O'Connor quotes Judith Herman, an authority on trauma, who states that a common reaction to trauma is to banish the traumatic events from consciousness. Certain experiences cannot be said aloud. They are truly "unspeakable." O'Connor describes denial as the psychological defense we use to protect our psyches and souls against suffering. Denial, even as it protects us, can become a way of living that inhibits human flourishing, cutting off the human spirit at its roots and denying a relationship with God's Spirit. Denial silences voices and blocks passions for justice.

In worship, your community can break its denial and amnesia, even if the community operates from a model of harmony and cooperation that ignores conflict, clashing interests, and past suffering. Many congregations do not feel the need to look at their past, but their past will not let them go. As a leader in your Gospel community, you are called to create the future vision they have for themselves as a community in the present. Truth(s) about the present and the past is a precondition for moving into the future.

The Book of Lamentations refuses denial, practices truth-telling, and reverses any amnesia, whether in the lives of individuals or in Gospel communities. It invites readers into communal and individual suffering. It sensitizes one to the pain that is present in the world.

Lamentations becomes a model for any steeple that cries. As the community remembers, it offers the first promise for healing since bringing grief into view is the very first step needed for restoration. The truth-telling of Lamentations's theology of witness offers hope for the body of Christ and comfort for a world that knows pain and suffering intimately.

Lamentations provides us with the following guidelines as we seek communion-as-the-work-of-mourning:

- The essence of doing the work of mourning is remembering and lamenting a past and a present

- The "unspeakable" is verbalized with the knowledge that no memory of the past or present understanding is complete.

- No single memory or vision of the past within a Gospel community may dominate that community. There are many memories, as varied as the church membership.

- The act of voicing a community's experiences in the presence of God is a sacred act, a visit to holy ground.

WORSHIP, LAMENT, AND THE WORK OF MOURNING

The powerful voice of Lamentations can lead us to think that boldly naming the realities of our congregations can be helpful. But be mindful. Barbara Lundblad, in her book *Transforming the Stone: Preaching through Resistance and Change* (2001), writes that calls for radical change may only increase the uncertainty many are experiencing.[44] She warns that a "fearful analysis" of a community's life—even when it is accurate—will be tuned out completely. Merely going into the pulpit and naming the losses the community is grieving can be a "fearful analysis" if conversation-as-the-work-of-mourning is not occurring. Lundblad's warning is not a call to remain silent about the inward experience of our communities. Rather, she states:

> If our preaching denies the fear, where will people go with their fears: the fear that everything is changing, the fear of those who are different,

the fear that others count more than they do, the fear that God himself is no longer Himself? *Fear unnamed does not go away. It lingers inside. It turns inward as depression or outward as verbal or physical violence. Transformation cannot happen if fears are discounted or denied.* (Emphasis added)[45]

Will you, narrative inquirer of your Gospel community and some- one well acquainted with your own work of mourning, foster commu- nal transformation by preaching about the inward uncertainty and confusion your community experiences when loss and change touch- es its life? As the prophet Isaiah states, you were anointed by God to enflesh good news, so that those stuck in the "ashes of mourning" can receive "oil of gladness" (Isa. 61:1–3). You are called to name the fears that your community experiences, thereby breaking down the silence that exists around hard things.

But how does one preach for transformation and facilitate com- munion-as-the-work-of mourning? Lundblad suggests that the start- ing point of preaching for transformation is sermons "grounded in grace." Drawing on the experience of Mary in Luke 1:47–53, she sees grace as God's reign that has come to earth and touched our everyday lives. Preaching about grace has to be made tangible, and it is always specific. It is bringing the assurance of God's presence in the midst of "ashes of mourning." Although a natural instinct might be to think that a focus on repentance or urging people to accept the changes that occurred will facilitate transformation, focusing on grace will create the space needed for the work of mourning to occur. Grace is that unexpected gift from God that interrupts grief and sustains the inten- tional process of moving beyond grief.

If grace is the starting point for preaching about transition, one pathway to follow as you lead your community in the work of mourn- ing is to follow the tradition of Psalms of Lament. Lament is the pat- tern of speech created by Israel to express their experience before God. As the communal expression of pain, suffering and loss, but also of trust and hope, lament defines much of communion-as-the-work- of-mourning. The basic intent of Israel's lament is to rehabilitate and restore those who are suffering, and the form of lament assists this intent.

In his book *Biblical Approaches to Pastoral Counseling* (1981), Donald Capps writes that lament enhances experience, brings to articulation, and limits the experience of suffering so that people can live with the losses and transitions.[46] The form of lament invites experiencing and understanding miseries, hurts, and agonies, and allows for the work of mourning to be done. In addition, as God listens to the suffering of God's people, God laments, too. In Jeremiah, for example, God's lament complements the lament of Jeremiah.

Many theologians, among them Kathleen Billman, Walter Brueggemann, Donald Capps, Kathleen O'Connor, Daniel Migliore, and Claus Westermann, argue for the reclamation of lament by the Christian church in the west.[47] Due to numerous forces, such as the longevity of human life, shifting theological trends, increased individuality in society, the advances of technical medicine, and a general denial of death and loss, lament is discouraged and avoided. With this loss of a tradition, the Christian church in Europe and North America has lost the transformative power of lament and the ability to fully embrace the changes that the body of Christ experiences. The lack of Psalms of Lament in our hymnals is but one example of where this loss manifests itself. Nearly one third of the Psalms are rarely read or sung.

The transformative power of a lament is not that it gives answers, but rather that we experience suffering again while we have a hearing. God listens. And when we voice our pain, fear, and trust before God, we are transformed. In the language of Bruce Reed, lament provides a Gospel community the opportunity to express its absolute dependence upon God and to identify with God, thereby inviting the community to refind a new identity.

For congregations experiencing change and loss, the Psalms of Lament become the inner voice of fear and uncertainty and the outward voice of trust and hope. The Psalms of Lament invite personal and communal identification with the emotional, relational, and spiritual worlds of the psalmist as the psalmist oscillates between feelings and faith. Psalms, such as Psalms 23, 32, and 37, are especially comforting resources to those who are frustrated, disillusioned, embittered, conscience-stricken, or fearful.

Psalms of Lament, both individual and communal, can be distinguished from psalms that express thanksgiving and praise, penitence, trust, or wisdom. They have a characteristic structure, which Capps summarizes as follows:

Address to God: The address to God is usually a brief cry for help, but is occasionally expanded to include a statement of praise or a recollection of God's intervention in the past (Ps. 71:1–3).

Complaint: God is informed about diverse problems or concerns that individuals or a community experience. In penitential psalms, the complaint can be the acknowledgment of one's sins (Ps. 71:4).

Confession of trust: The psalmist proclaims confidence in God despite the circumstances and begins to see his or her problems differently (Ps. 71:5–8).

Petition: Having expressed confidence in God, the psalmist appeals to God for deliverance and intervention. The petitioner might express reasons why God should intervene, ranging from the petitioner's confession of guilt or innocence to God's faithfulness in the past (Ps. 71:9–13).

Words of assurance: The psalmist expresses certainty that the petition will be heard by God (Ps. 71:14a).

Vow of praise: The lament concludes with the psalmist's vow to witness to God's intervention (Ps. 71:14b–24).

Whether it is a personal or a communal lament, most often we do not know the circumstances that prompted the lament. Scholars believe that this was not mere oversight on the part of the psalmist, but the unknown circumstances allow for a "companionship of feelings." The psalmist's failure to be factual enables us to identify with the original lamenter. This identification with the powerful emotions within a Psalm of Lament becomes a source of transformation and healing for individuals and Gospel communities even today.

Claus Westermann identifies a specific variation on the Psalm of Lament, which he calls "the lament of the mediator."[48] Here, a person does not bring his or her personal losses before God, but through mediation brings the suffering of a community before God. Moses,

Elisha, and Jeremiah are examples of leaders who lamented Israel's oppression in Egypt or their sinful wander from God. The lament of the mediator is prophetic in nature. As experienced by the prophets, the suffering of others impacts the mediator. The person's accusation against God becomes an accusation against the mediator. The cry of Jesus on the cross stands in continuity with this tradition of lament. In form and function, the lament of the mediator is the same as the Psalms of Lament discussed above.

For you as a church leader, this means that you can mediate the lament of your community. But as your community complains before God, some of their anger and resentment can be directed towards you. You become a "suffering servant" not unlike the suffering servant in Deutero-Isaiah.

Pastor Lanz experienced "the lament of the mediator" as a painful but necessary experience. He became the pastor of a congregation that lost their previous pastor under suspicious circumstances. There were rumors of sexual misconduct, but nobody knew for certain. The loss of trust the community experienced in their pastoral leader was obvious, and as Pastor Lanz attempted to give voice to the distrust and underlying hostility present in the community, he experienced how people directed their hostility towards him. His supervisor encouraged him to continue his conversations with his parishioners about what the previous pastor meant to them. He heard that he was a beloved pastor who suddenly left without explanation and without giving the community the chance to end their relationship with him. Pastor Lanz, in turn, lamented the fact that he receives anger that is "unfairly" directed at him. This lament made it possible for him to remain present to his community. Over the months the desire of the community to talk about the previous pastor diminished, and Pastor Lanz felt more accepted by the members. Pastor Lanz could have written his very own Psalm of Lament.

If it is the formfulness of lament (Walter Brueggemann), its structure, that facilitates the grieving process, how can you as a leader of your Gospel community shape your sermon or whole worship service according to the form of lament? Your sermon, for example, can mirror the elements of a lament even if your Scripture of the day is not a Psalm of Lament:

- Address to God

  Address God, whether implicit or explicit. Initiate the movement out of your community's stage of realization and relative independence. Accept your role and function as a mediator of lament. Example: "Our help is in the name of the Lord, who made heaven and earth. Amen" (Ps. 124:8).

- Complaint

  Name with a deep sense of trust the transitions and losses experienced by your Gospel community. The complaint is the language of suffering and discomfort. If your congregation is experiencing a fruitful period, name the transitions and their impact on the community with gratitude. Move towards the expression of absolute dependence on God.

- Confession of trust

  Your community experiences trust when their spiritual and emotional reactions to change and loss—fear, uncertainty, anger, confusion, hope, joy, or gratitude—are named in God's presence; when the body of Christ is invited to share each other's burdens. Here the community says: "Our complaint notwithstanding, we will praise God." The confession of trust, as can be seen in the confession of our sins, is an expression of absolute dependence upon God.

- Petition

  Petition God's assistance as your community works through the powerful spiritual, emotional, and relational reactions to transition and as it lives into a new identity. Provide new symbols from Scripture (a tree that flourishes, a ruin being rebuilt, etc.) that can inform the identity of your community. It is also an indirect expression of absolute dependence upon God. Here you name the work of mourning.

- Words of assurance

  Express assurance that God hears the lament of God's people and that the community is supporting and praying for each other.

Initiate the move back to a new phase of realization.

• Vow of praise

Express praise and gratitude for God's faithful presence in your community, even as your community is experiencing painful or difficult transitions. Praise is the language of joy. End your sermon or worship with a new position of realization and relative independence.

The expression of lament is vital for the body of Christ and is facilitative of the work of mourning. *Have you ever written a Psalm of Lament?* Drafting a lament is a life-giving and life-affirming task not only for the leaders of Gospel communities, but for the communities themselves. As you write your lament to assist the work of mourning, Capps reminds his readers to keep the following in mind:

• Do draft the complaint mindful of the range and depth of the emotional, spiritual, and relational reaction to change. Address the anger, guilt, frustration, and disillusionment, but also the feelings of trust, self-justification, and defending the integrity of one's actions that are often experienced in grief.

• Do petition God to intervene in your community, and do not confuse petitioning God with a refusal to accept the losses or changes that occurred. To petition God is not an attempt to bargain with God (Elizabeth Kübler-Ross), but rather it is the legitimate expression of seeking help. Petitioning God awakens new spiritual energies to overcome the loss and transition.

• Do express words of assurance that follow the petition. Here you enter into a priestly and mediating role as you communicate the experience of God's trustworthiness. Communicate that God seeks restoration and fruitfulness for your Gospel community. To help the Gospel community with this, God has sent his Comforter.

• Do express a vow of praise to testify to what God has done in your community. Capps reminds us that praise is the final move within the form of a lament and that expressing praise can be difficult for the community if they do not understand God's role in the loss and transition they are experiencing. Central to this understanding is that God is grieving, too; that God laments ("God, you who lament the losses we named in your presence . . .").

As you write a lament for your community possibly in collaboration with members of your community, the following communal Psalms of Lament can guide your thinking: Psalm 12; 44; 58; 60; 74; 79; 80; 83; 85; 90; 94; 123; 126; 137. Individual Psalms of Lament can be informative to Gospel communities as well: 3; 5–7; 9; 10; 13; 17; 22; 25; 26; 27; 28; 31; 35; 38; 39; 40; 42; 43; 51; 54–57; 59; 61; 63; 64; 60–71; 77; 86; 88; 102; 109; 120; 130; 140–43. Some of these psalms are penitential in nature, such as Psalm 51. Others are cursing or imprecatory psalms, such as Psalm 12, while other psalms are protestations of innocence, such as Psalm 44.

Writing one's own prayer of lament can be a powerful experience. Here are two examples of Psalms of Lament written by pastors. The first lament is of a pastor currently serving as an associate pastor at a wealthy historic Gospel community. For this pastor, living into his call means that he often laments his ministry and the lives of his community and denomination.

A PSALM OF LAMENT

O Lord, you are the God of our ancestors.
You are our God before our birth,
even before time began.

You built your Church and opened her doors, O Lord.
You blessed your church and gave her life.
You gave her a voice.

Have you forgotten your Church O God,
have you left her to fend for herself?
Lord, hear us in our pain and fear.

We see young people walking the streets,
yet we do not see them in our churches.
We remember friends, who have left us.
We remember friends, who have forgotten us.

Now our churches sit empty.
Doors shut like a coffin,
our sorrow increases with each nail driven.

We have invited people to join us,
yet silence fills our ears, and emptiness surrounds us.
Why are we alone?

O Lord, where is our voice,
will anyone still listen?
The hymns are not sung,
the creeds are not confessed,
the Word falls on deaf ears.

We preach your Gospel,
we serve your world,
we try to hold to what you taught us.
Where is our voice? Will no one listen!

Our nation marches to war as we cry "Peace!"
Our churches only seem to matter when buildings fall.
People only need us to marry and bury them.

We were once a church of tradition and pride,
we were once a church of scholars and thinkers.
We were once a church with renowned preachers.

At one time we were blessed,
at one time, we had influence,
at one time, we mattered.

Have we wronged you?
Have we not sung your praise?
Have we not been faithful with what you gave us?

Lord, we are a confused people,
Lord, we have forgotten your goodness,
Lord, we have taken our own path.

O Lord, you choose us, we did not choose you.
We are your people, and you will not abandon us.
Set our feet upon the path again.

Bring life to us again.
Lord once again fill the churches
with people seeking to praise you.
Lord bring the next generation
to meet you in our midst.
Return our voice, that we may once again,
spread the Gospel of your love.

Help us to be faithful,
help us to seek you,
help us find ourselves in your presence.

We will continue to praise you,
we will continue to worship you,
when our hearts are sad
and when they are filled with joy.

Great are you, O Lord
Now and forever more.

Another pastor, who serves an emerging church in a mid-size city, wrote this lament about his ministry:

CREATOR GOD . . . A PSALM OF LAMENT

Sin hunts me like a dog
So quickly it pursues me I can barely catch my breath
My lungs ache, my legs tire, and I will soon drop
I can hear it panting as it comes up behind me
You do nothing

Around every turn and every bend death awaits
Crouching like a tiger,
Yet you see it, I see it, it doesn't need to hide
Because you do nothing

If my earthly father saw my life so close to ruin
Surely he would step in, or maybe not
Are you no better than him?
Why do you do nothing?

You are my creator God
You are my King
You are my Lord
You may be my Savior
You are not my Father . . . or maybe you are

Three times I pleaded with you to take it away
Three times you said, my grace is sufficient
What the hell does that mean?

My passion is to know Christ in his death and resurrection
So, about the loneliness and affliction I can't complain
But the sin?

Do not let my enemy destroy me Lord
Which it seems it is so close to doing
And how about a little resurrection?
Or must I first die. Do you enjoy death?

It is for freedom Christ has set us free . . .
Then why am I in bondage?
Why won't you answer me?
I quit, condemned to hell,
Do what you want, you will anyway

Be my father
I need a father
I can't find you
I don't even know who you are
Please come quickly

Peace out Yo

For many leaders of Gospel communities, writing a lament about the disappointments of their ministry is an important task as they live into their call. Can these modern laments be an inspiration for you to write your own? Or to gather members of your community to write one for the community? Likewise, lament as a creative response to loss and transition can facilitate the work of mourning in your congregation. Imagine educating the groups used to engage in conversation-as-the-work-of-mourning on the formfulness of lament and then asking them to write a communal lament. These laments are all assembled; each week one is inserted with the church bulletin or newsletter, or you can use them as the prayer of the people. The ritual of writing a lament will facilitate communion-as-the-work-of-mourning.

Does writing a lament sound too frightening or risky to give it an honest try? Despite the theological, spiritual, emotional, and relational importance of lament, your congregation might find the writing of a communal lament a difficult task. Some members of your community will no doubt resist communion-as-the-work-of-mourning. Walter Brueggemann wants to comfort us as we embrace lament when he writes with encouragement and optimism about the reclamation of lament. In an essay called "Necessary Conditions for a Good Loud Lament," he traces how the tradition of Psalms of Lament was lost in the light of the Enlightenment's self-confidence.[49] Self-sufficiency, a key marker of our society, does not encourage lament. Brueggemann's tone in the essay is optimistic, however, since he sees that in recent years the community of faith has begun to remember what it had all but forgotten. He envisions a leadership that is intentional, interpretive, and instructional as they create the evangelical context in which the transformative power of lament can be embraced. Brueggemann gives ten preconditions and prerequisites for the recovery of lament. For Gospel communities seeking communion-as-the-work-of-mourning, the ten conditions for expressing lament can be restated as follows:

+ + +

PRECONDITIONS FOR LAMENT

1. Your community is admitting its self-sufficiency, self-invention, and self-actualization before God, who can be addressed and who listens.

2. As leaders you have a growing awareness of how the power and control that is inherent in your role can either inhibit or facilitate conversation and dialogue around difficult issues.

3. Your community is embracing a moral universe where God invites the lonely outsider, now living in a world of the strong, the quick, and the well-connected, and of restraints, judgment, and lack of norms, into community.

4. Your community is accepting of its existence as the body of Christ, a body whose source of life is not finances.

5. Your community is remembering its past and engages tradition.

6. Your community is encouraging the voicing of pain and suffering and is overcoming the silence and conformity that pervades our culture.

7. Your community is transcending the radical individualism of our age.

8. Your community is creating space for the inevitable anxiety a com

9. Your community is becoming a truth-telling, memory-cherishing, and hope-practicing community.

10. Your community is anticipating the miraculous intervention by God as the Gospel community is revitalized and restored.

+ + +

How do you evaluate your community vis-à-vis these ten state-ments that are prerequisites for the reclamation of lament? Some com-munities need to further engage in conversation-as-the-work-of-mourning as the community is educated and empowered to accept the invitation of restoration within lament. Bringing lament into your experience of worship, as this chapter encourages, will inform and instruct your community, cultivating the preconditions mentioned here. Besides preaching, however, worshiping God is also done through music, prayers, the sacraments, and bringing offerings. In the remainder of this chapter, these various components are briefly addressed.

THE MUSIC OF MOURNING AS A TRANSITIONAL EXPERIENCE

Dietrich Bonhoeffer once said that "music is completely the servant of the Word."[50] Music plays an important role in the experience of wor-ship. It facilitates the oscillation process as the Gospel community is invited on a pilgrimage from living a life of relative independence to expressing absolute dependence on God and moving back to a newly defined relative independence. Music assists continuity and change. If lament is central to communion-as-the-work-of-mourning, so too is the music of worship. Sadly, however, Psalms of Lament are absent in most hymnals and are thus rarely sung by congregations. *In an age of praise choruses, how can music facilitate the work of mourning? How can you have liturgical integrity if your music does not speak to the sorrow and uncertainty your Gospel community is experiencing?*

Paul Pruyser, a psychologist, writes about music as a dynamic and imaginative experience that can help us process life. For Pruyser, singing a funeral dirge, for example, leads people out of their deeply personal world of sorrow (which he calls their "autistic world") to a world where the imagination and hope can function (the "illusionistic world").[51] Music is transitional since it leads us between different realities of self, other, and the imaginative (the in-between). Likewise, music is transformational, since it can alter our self-experience.

Pruyser refers to Augustine who wrote in his *Confessions* that Bishop Ambrose of Milan instigated congregational singing in his church because he saw the sorrow of his community. Music was not used to deafen the bishop to the sorrow of church members but rather facilitated mourning. Bishop Ambrose knew that singing hymns and psalms would transpose their sorrow to oil of gladness (Isa. 61: 2–3).

A challenge awaits a Gospel community that only sings praise choruses. Despite contemporary Christian music's rapid development and rise in popularity, few artists write songs that can be described as a modern lament. Some artists writing popular Christian music, such as Don Francisco, Tim Hughes, John Michael Talbot, Ten Shekel Shirt, and Tommy Walker, do explore lament and the psalms in contemporary music. The Wild Goose Resource Group of the Iona Community in Scotland (with John Bell and Kathy Galloway) also provides contemporary resources to address mourning and lament. If your community worships in a contemporary style, you need to discern how your music is facilitating community-as-the-work-of-mourning.

Within traditional hymnody, many hymns and psalms can facilitate communion-as-the-work-of-mourning. Your music director can be a great resource to you as you structure your worship service. Do educate your music director about the oscillation process within worship and on the importance of music as people are invited to do their personal and communal work of mourning. Music not only creates the atmosphere that makes the work of mourning possible, but it becomes an agent of healing and transformation. Here I merely highlight a few hymns that will speak to the sorrow and uncertainty your Gospel community is experiencing in times of loss and transition. A musician in my Gospel community introduced me to the work of Brian Wren.[52]

When joy is drowned in heartbreak and dejection
That gives no guarantee of resurrection
We struggle to retain
The echo of Christ's name

Though hope runs dry, and faith gives no protection.

We cannot speed the moment of our waking
By rage, or acts of will to stem the aching
But only recognize a stillness of surprise
When clouds have passed, and dawn at last is breaking.

Another Wren hymn, "When pain and sorrow strike by chance," addresses the spiritual and emotional response to crisis or change. Here Wren identifies the search for the "dominant other:"[53]

When pain and terror strike by chance,
With causes unexplained,
When God seems absent or asleep, and evil unrestrained,
We crave an all controlling force ready to rule and warn,
But find, far overshadowed, by a cross,
A child in weakness born.

Since wisdom took its chance on earth,
To show God's loving way,
We'll trust that fear and force will fail, and wisdom wins the day,
Then, come, dear Christ, and hold us fast when faith and hope are torn,
And bring us in your loving arms,
To resurrection morn.

The Wild Goose Resource Group has a short hymn describing the conduct within a Gospel community as conversation and compassion-as-the-work-of-mourning is done. It is called "For Such a Time as This:"[54]

For such a time as this, we are called to commitment.
For such a time as this, we are called to the struggle,
Sometimes to listen, sometimes to weep, sometimes to risk or to speak.
Called to be caring, called to act, for such a time as this.

Most hymnals contain at least a few Psalms of Lament or other hymns that can facilitate the work of mourning. Your music director should be able to identify such songs for you. If your congregation's music style reflects more of a "praise and worship" character, then the music of Tim Hughes can provide you with choruses that addresses lament.[55] His song "Whole World in His Hands," from the CD "When Silence Falls," leads us to sing:

> When all around is fading, when nothing seems to last,
> When each day is filled with sorrow, still I know with all my heart,
> He's got the whole world in his hands,
> He's got the whole world in his hands,
> I fear no evil, for You are with me.
> Strong to deliver, Mighty to save,
> He's got the whole world in his hands.
>
> When I walk through fire, I will not be burnt,
> When the woes come crashing 'round me, still I know with all my heart,
> He's got the whole world in his hands.

His song, "When the Tears Fall," also expresses lament and hope:

> I've had questions without answers,
> I've known sorrow, I've known pain.
> But there's one thing that I'll cling to,
> You are faithful, Jesus. You're true.
> When hope is lost, I'll call You Savior,
> When pain surrounds, I'll call You Healer,
> When silence falls, You'll be the song within my heart.
> In the lone hour of my sorrow, Through the darkest night of my soul,
> You surround me and sustain me, My Defender, evermore.

WHEN A GOSPEL COMMUNITY PRAYS

In her book *Standing in the Circle of Grief* (2002), Blair Gilmer Meeks states that when we pray in community, we not only acknowledge the reality of loss and suffering in our lives, but we also acknowledge the certainty that God has raised Christ from the dead and that God has the power to bring restoration and new life.[56] There is nothing illusionary or wishful about prayer, even if we use our capacity to imagine in order to hope. Rather, prayer gives us the opportunity to express with honesty our deepest experiences before our Lord as we realize our mortality and the brokenness of our reality. Whether your community's need is seeking guidance, or comfort, or faith, or revitalization, or to express their gratitude and joy, you can bring the community's needs before God's throne in prayer.

Prayer in community, however, can be manipulative and irresponsible if you have not had a conversation about the content of the prayer. You can run the risk that your prayer will become a monologue wrapped in pastoral authority and power. No one in your community may stand up and scream out as you pray "No, it isn't so!" if your prayer does not reflect the spiritual, emotional, and relational milieu of your community. Praying in community naturally follows conversation-as-the-work-of-mourning since you can verbalize the sorrow, uncertainty, or gratitude your community experiences.

Kathleen Billman and Daniel Migliore, in their book *Rachel's Cry: Prayer of Lament and the Rebirth of Hope* (1999), state that congregations need to include prayers of lament in their worship to avoid becoming "shallow and evasive."[57] Of course, not all expression of lament automatically leads to revitalization, but a core message in Scripture is that God is at work in moments of dis-ease, fear, and yearning.

Billman and Migliore identify two voices we can use when we pray: a summer voice (Ps. 150:6, "Let everything that has breath praise the Lord") and a winter voice (Ps. 130:1, "Out of the depths I cry to you, o Lord"). These two voices that belong together and cannot be separated describe the intricate balance between pain and praise and between penitence and celebration. *When you pray for your community, what voice do you use?* Do you find, as do some leaders of Gospel communities, that the more they are aware of the "winter moments" in their congregation, the stronger their "summer voice" becomes? The illusion that we can undo fear and uncertainty, even pain and suffering through praise only and by avoiding voicing the "winter moments," is pervasive and powerful.

The authors of *Rachel's Cry* say that the liturgy used by a congregation indicates the spiritual health of a congregation. What then, they ask, is the spiritual health of a congregation when lament is noticeably absent in the worship services of most Gospel communities? Of course

North American society carries ambivalent attitudes toward lament and the expression of grief, rage, and other "negative" emotions. Despite the fact that Billman and Migliore identify much reason to prompt a lament (wars, AIDS, famine, the plight of inner cities, the abuse of the environment and natural disasters), "we seem bereft of the intellectual and spiritual resources to come creatively with the experience of loss of power and prestige or the burning resentment that persists after experiences of abuse and oppression."[58] Despite the fears that some may have, prayers of lament do not lead to a "culture of complaint," nor do they feed the fear and uncertainty that are present. Lament will not fuel the radical individualism of our age.

If lament was encouraged by the hymns you have sung, and if it was present in your sermon, it flows naturally that your prayers will lament the present realities of your Gospel community. As I've stated, worship leaders abuse their privilege to be their community's voice before God if their prayer does not reflect a prior conversation. This is especially the situation with a prayer of lament, since lament awakens powerful ambivalent feelings in most people.

Prayer, too, functions as a transitional experience. It bridges our reality with the reality that God is preparing with and for us. A prayer of lament can span the chasm between a Gospel community's uncertainty and hostility on the one hand, and hope and faith on the other. In addition, prayer of lament promotes solidarity with those who suffer, a theme that is explored further in the next chapter.

What would a prayer of lament in the worship service look like? Below is a prayer, based on one written by Blair Meeks, called "Great is thy Faithfulness: A Responsive Prayer." It was prayed in a Gospel community that is experiencing a rapid increase in membership. The rapid increase changed their identity in an unrecognizable manner, bringing much tension to the community. One of the significant losses they experienced was the loss of farmland. They lost their "neighborhood" as farmland was developed into homes and apartment complexes. The prayer attempted to bridge the ambivalence present in many members who mourned the changes in the congregation, even as they wanted to be welcoming to new members. Some new members, however, were resentful towards the "old members" because they could sense the hostility directed towards them. The prayer was drafted after much conversation in small groups over a seven-week period. During the time, the pastor preached the Exodus narrative. Can you use this prayer as a model prayer to lament authentically the reality of your Gospel community?

GREAT IS YOUR FAITHFULNESS:

A RESPONSIVE PRAYER

> My soul is bereft of peace;
> I have forgotten what happiness is; . . .
> But this I call to mind,
> and therefore I have hope:
> The steadfast love of the LORD never ceases,
> God's mercies never come to an end;
> They are new every morning;
> Great is your faithfulness.
>   (Lam. 3:17, 22–23)

O God, we have seen our membership, our identity, and our neighborhood changing. Even as we bow down low; we do not know who we are. Turn our minds toward you and grant us grace to remember your steadfast love.

Great is your faithfulness, O God our Savior.

All that is around us mourns: the farms are no more, the animals of the fields have left. We grieve alone, for we do not know each other's names. Who we are becoming remains uncertain. Turn our minds toward you and grant us grace to remember your steadfast love.

Great is your faithfulness, O God our Savior.

God, we are living like a Moses of old, who traveled to a promised land. We are walled in by our grief for what we have left behind, shaken by the uncertainty of what is to come. Who will comfort us? Who will give us rest? Yet we experience the joy for and the gifts of new members, new families, and new ministries. How can we express our gratitude for these blessings even as we do our work of mourning? Turn our minds toward you and grant us grace to remember your steadfast love.

Great is your faithfulness, O God our Savior.

We cry out in the night; we pour out our hearts like water before your presence. Hear our cry; take our lifted hands. Let us remember those who left and the traditions we lost. Accept our gratitude. Let us be welcoming to our new brothers and sisters. Turn our minds toward you and grant us grace to remember your steadfast love.

Great is your faithfulness, O God our Savior.

We call on your name, O Lord, from the depths of our sorrow and uncertainty. We long to hear your voice. Turn your face toward us that we may live in the light of your steadfast love.

Great is your faithfulness, O God our Savior.

Take up our cause, O God, and give us a new identity, new vision, and new mission. How can we be your Body in this developing community? Scatter the anxiety that causes hostility and that stop our prayers. Turn your face toward us that we may live in the light of your steadfast love.

Great is your faithfulness, O God our Savior.

Remember, O Lord, what has happened and is happening to us. Come near to us that we may hear you when you say, "Do not be afraid." Turn your face toward us that we may live in the light of your steadfast love.

Great is your faithfulness, O God our Savior.

Keep restoring us to yourself, O Lord, that we may be restored. Grant us your tender mercies, new every morning. Our hope is in you, for you have redeemed our life, and you will reign forever. Your steadfast love never ceases.

Great is your faithfulness, O God our Savior. Amen.

Pray this prayer or a similar prayer slowly so that you do not rush over loss. Prayers can be powerful moments within communion-as-the-work-of-mourning. To make them such, you need to spend time in conversation with members of your Gospel community. Invite members of your community who engaged in conversation-as-the-work-of-mourning to draft the prayer with you. The power of prayer can span different realties and can alter the self-expression of your Gospel community.

RITUALS CAN FACILITATE THE WORK OF MOURNING

Rituals, those prescribed symbolic acts that are performed during moments of separation, threshold or liminal moments, and moments of reincorporation, "assist us in moving through life's painful losses as well as deepening our experience of our joys. Good rituals can help us move from one place to another in life. They can help us overcome the 'stuckness' of experiences, attitudes, or circumstances that seem to hold onto us and keep us from moving ahead."[59]

In Chapter 1, Pastor Lou ritualized the memory of his Gospel community. The essence of the ritual was that they would bring artifacts to place on a table remembering the life of the community. Whether a person brought an item to place on the table or not, people would invariably walk up to the table, look at the photographs, read the materials left behind, and touch some of the artifacts. By allowing themselves to remember the past they had with the congregation, the members of Pastor Lou's community did the work of mourning.

Communion-as-the-work-of-mourning includes numerous rituals that can facilitate mourning and open self and soul for transitions. Some of the rituals are: the experience of worship itself; the liturgy that gives structure to worship; performing a baptism, Holy Communion or a funeral; or, structuring a ritual specifically to facilitate the work of mourning.

Erik Erikson states that rituals, even the ones we learn in early childhood play activity, are central to our lives.[60] They connect our personal worlds with the world out there. Most of us, Erikson writes, are "caught between the wish to look backward and the necessity to look ahead."[61] Erikson identifies the deep human need for a context that makes meaningful all other contexts and that gives a perspective from which to view all of reality. We ritualize our daily lives to gain perspective. Surely, worship is also such a context. Rituals, Erikson writes, accomplish a number of things, some of which are:[62]

- Ritual elevates personal needs into a broader communal context.

- Ritual transforms a sense of personal omnipotence to a joint sense of destiny.

- Ritual informs outward behavior.

- Ritual facilitates the development of identity.

- Ritual facilitates a general shared vision for a community.

Shared visions refer to the conscious and unconscious visual imagery that comes to our minds when we engage in ritual. The rituals we bring into worship, whether the sacraments or other, provide pictures of faith and life, even an ecclesiology. In "shared vision," "I" become a "we" or an "us."

The seminary where I teach has daily chapel services. A number of years ago, we started practicing the ritual of Holy Communion every Friday. The attendance for this service is double or more compared to the Monday through Thursday attendance. As a faculty, we often talk about the unifying effect of the Friday service and how ritual centers our community even as we are growing rapidly as a school and as a community of scholars. We experience the power of ritual's "shared visions," that rituals bring hope and "arouse productive and communal energy in the greatest variety of individuals at a given moment in history."[63] Likewise, the rituals of worship provide a countervision to the visions that are communicated by culture and the dynamics of loss and change.

We were created to have the capacity for play and ritual. Two persons who have addressed the intricate connection between story, ritual, and the human brain are David Hogue and Peter Atkins.[64] Hogue, a theologian and counselor, examines living "on the cusp between the past and the future" and explores in ways Erikson could not do, due to the incomplete knowledge of neuroscience Erikson had, the ways we live between the past that formed us for better or worse and the future we can imagine and hope for. Whereas Hogue writes with pastoral care in mind, Atkins, a retired Anglican bishop, writes explicitly thinking about the liturgies you and I create in worship. Atkins and Hogue agree that worship's effectiveness is determined by the brain's preferences for linkages, association of ideas, and its search for completion. In communion-as-the-work-of-mourning we receive information in word and action that we are valued, cared for, and loved, and that the appropriate response is thanksgiving, acceptance, and worshiping God. Our brains then establish memory patterns that determine helpful behavior.[65]

Like you and me, your community is also driven by memory and imagination. And in worship, memory, story, and imagination come together. Here, as in many other moments in life, what is meets what was and what could be. Perception meets memory and imagination. Without memory there can be no worshiping God. When your Gospel community opts for nostalgia, they are not really remembering, but they are pining for a past in such a way that it shapes memory by detaching memory from the context of your community. In nostalgia there is more emotional investment than reality. At best, it is highly selective remembering.

Narratives and rituals, however, speak beyond nostalgia and thoughts. They communicate powerfully to our senses and our emotions. In a culture that puts much emphasis on the development of the mind, the members of your Gospel community may not have the ability to access the sorrow, fear, and uncertainty they experience as the community finds itself in a transitional period. Or it can be that your experience of worship relies on only the cognitive abilities we carry as no other senses are addressed. In worship, you can create a holding environment (see Chapter 1) where your community can acknowledge their emotional presence before God. The tradition of lament will play a central role in expressing sorrow and uncertainty, but also hope and trust in God. Interestingly, Hogue also indicates the relationship between stories, rituals, our brains, and the ability to express empathy towards people and care towards the earth. The narratives and rituals you bring into worship will facilitate compassion-as-the-work-of-mourning. The way we listen to a narrative in worship is the same way we probably listen in other settings.

Each member, however, will hear a narrative or experience a ritual in a personal way. Since each member of your Gospel community is in a different place vis-à-vis the transitions the community is experiencing, a wide range of emotions is experienced within a community that is in grief. Often leaders are uncertain how to engage a group who might be angry and filled with sadness if another group is actually grateful that the changes are occurring. Some persons are still angry and resentful, while others have completed some work of mourning and have moved on. The power of narratives and rituals transcend these differences even if sometimes you need to structure worship to address the spiritual place of only a certain group of people in your community.

For all participating in worship, telling the stories of your community and of God's pilgrimage with God's people is healing, but it also makes the rewriting of your community's stories or the discovery of a new story possible. Lifting up the experiences of your community in God's presence communicates the importance of the life of the community and it provides structure and order to the experience that your community is having.

Your community already has numerous rituals: for birth, marriage, death, installing persons into office, to greet each other, and more. A certain congregation always ends their worship with the community professing "Jesus is Lord" while they hold one hand up. The community, which has been going through significant leadership changes and intrapsychic and systemic losses for some years, is "held," in part, by this ritual. Since your community already relies on rituals to structure its life, the ground has been prepared for using rituals to facilitate the work of mourning. Both the work of mourning and the use of narratives and rituals imply that we remember and imagine so that we can make sense of what happened and what is to come. Drawing on the works of Peter Atkins and David Hogue, keep the following guidelines in mind as you prepare to use narrative and rituals in your congregation:

- Plan, prepare, and perform the ritual with anticipation.
- Draft the narratives and rituals you will use in advance and always in collaboration with other members of your community.
- Keep the narratives short and the ritual simple.
- Narratives and ritual communicate values. Be clear as to what they are.
- Narratives and ritual need to give space for the influence of emotion and sensory stimulation (smell, touch, taste, sight, and hearing).
- Discern the timing of and accents within narratives and ritual. Both can combine time zones. Remember that narratives and ritual are primarily about a current status, not so much about a past event.
- Choose language for your narrative or acts for your ritual with which your community can identify. Provide vivid images, whether from Scripture (the Exodus narrative, for example) or the life of your community (what was, what is, and what is becoming).
- Remember that the human mind is wired to imagine and imitate. Allow time for personal reflection. Imitation is strengthened by repetition. Do not change your entire worship liturgy from week to week.
- Engage in conversation after the worship to discern the meaningfulness of the experience. Narratives and rituals can bring confusion as well as clarity.
- Rituals are powerful experiences of transformation. Be inviting and permission-giving, rather than manipulative and coercive.

In my tradition, baptism is portrayed in covenantal language and the Lord's Supper is described as "a feast of remembrance, communion, and of hope." Both sacraments reiterate Gods faithfulness to God's people through all the ages. Being mindful of the role and function of the sacraments can facilitate the work of mourning in your community. .

COMMUNION-AS-THE-WORK-OF-MOURNING DURING THE CHURCH YEAR

Use the church calendar to address the "seasons" of your Gospel community's life. Advent highlights the theme of longing, whereas Christmas can focus on joy, gratitude, and the displacement of Jesus. During Epiphany, wander with the Magi, and in the season of Lent, repent the ways your community has neglected the body of Christ and lament its sinful nature, prone to bring division and conflict.

On Good Friday, remember the mourners, those who remember a previous time, and resist rushing to Easter. During Easter, embrace the promise of God's blessing for a new life even as we continue to live in the tension between the "already" and the "not yet." Ascension reminds us of Christ's Lordship over the church, but also that we are the ones without a home. Lastly, Pentecost presents the assurance of a future promise. Of course other days in the year, such as All Saints's Day, also present opportunities to do the communal work of mourning.

As a leader in your Gospel community, you have the pastoral authority to "use" the experiences of worship to facilitate the work of mourning in your community. This use of worship, which should not be confused with the "exploitation" of worship, is being responsible with the opportunities God provides to facilitate and transform the life of your congregation.

CONCLUSION

Communion-as-the-work-of-mourning revisits the foundations of our relationship with God; we connect with God's character and being and with the body of Christ; we explore the truths about our current context, our past, and our future; and, we create new memories of how God interacts with us. In communion-as-the-work-of-mourning, especially as it is expressed in the lament tradition of Scripture, we foster a new community and open new vistas of being the body of Christ at this time and in this place. God becomes present as the One who saves.

Doing communal work of mourning is not easier than doing our individual work. Naming the losses and transitions a community experiences in a worship context is difficult, but so too would be silence, or absence, or a refusal to address the sorrow and grief that is in your Gospel community. Sometimes these changes are named with the same hesitation and certainty that are within loss and mourning. Bringing lament into worship is a creative act that goes beyond theology, since theology has a tendency to objectify God. Loss is not an issue to be addressed; it can only be acknowledged in persons. This chapter focused on two books only, the Book of Lamentations and the Psalms. You are, however, not restricted to these books when you want to encourage your community to lament. Draw on the personal and communal laments in the other books of Scripture, such as The Exodus, Ezra, Nehemiah, The Book of Job, Isaiah, Jeremiah, Hosea, and Joel, to name just a few.

Worship, through narrative, song, and ritual, becomes a powerful activity that both confirms and resists the spiritual, emotional, relational, and other contexts your Gospel community is occupying. The communion of a Gospel community carries the emotional potential to accept and transform the losses the congregation is experiencing. It instills and strengthens faith and leads to joy, a deeper emotion than happiness. A major aspect of this potential is to empower the members of the congregation you serve to enter into the next oscillation movement of relative independence, which includes being the hands and feet of Christ in the world.

Communal lament implores God to be compassionate to those who suffer. It is an appeal to God's compassion. Erikson forewarns us, however, that a ritual such as worship might actually bring tension between people, as it can identify those "who are excluded or exclude themselves from knowing the right way."[66] The final chapter embraces this risk by identifying a community of compassion and care as inherent to doing the work of mourning even if compassion and hospitality remain threatening experiences for many Gospel communities.

+ CHAPTER FIVE +

Compassion-as-the-work-of-mourning

Praise be to the God of our Lord Jesus Christ, the God of compassion and the God of all comfort, who comforts us in all our troubles, so that we can comfort those in any trouble with the comfort we ourselves have received from God.

(2 Cor. 1: 3b–4)

THIS FINAL CHAPTER IDENTIFIES PARTICIPATION in compassionate ministries as a central task of doing the work of mourning. From the Latin words *pati* and *cum*, "to suffer with," compassion means to be with a person or group, to hurt or feel with them, to take in their suffering as if it is your own. Being compassionate facilitates healing and restoration for all involved. Our culture sadly understands compassion as little more than pity or feeling sorry for someone. Jesus' ministry, however, was not pitiful; he suffered for and with us.

As I stated, the work of mourning requires that your Gospel community experiences living into a new identity. I believe that being hospitable and compassionate towards each other, towards persons and families not members of your community, and even towards nature implies living into being the body of Christ. Compassion is rooted deep in our relationship with God, the hospitable Host who prepares a table for us and helps us to see our enemies through new eyes (Ps. 23).

The apostle Paul describes God's compassion in the opening sentences of his second letter to the Corinthians:

Praise be to the God of our Lord Jesus Christ, the God of compassion and the God of all comfort, who comforts us in all our troubles, *so that we can comfort those in any trouble with the comfort we ourselves have received from God* (2 Cor. 1: 3b–4; emphasis added).

The Gospel community in the wealthy cosmopolitan city of Corinth was characterized by hostile disputes, making it impossible for them to function as the body of Christ. Paul reminds the believers in Corinth that they had received mercy and compassion from God. He encourages them to portray compassion even as they are persecuted and face persecution for their belief in Christ. Paul's argument is clear: When we encounter a compassionate God, the space is created that makes compassion to others possible.

In the first chapter I asked how your compassionate sacred heart shows in your ministry. I referred to two professors of business administration, Ronald Heifetz and Marty Linsky, who identified compassion as a key trait that effective leaders possess. I hope that engaging in conversation-as-the-work-of-mourning and communion-as-the-work-of-mourning awakened your compassionate heart. Without compassion the conversation would have died down and you would not have been able to authentically bring your community's lament into worship. The power of believing in the Incarnate One is that in the face of sadness and sorrow we discover the face of God.

Peace Church has not lived into its name since its senior pastor was asked to leave the congregation. He left under a cloud of controversy, and due to legal proceedings, much of the facts remain unknown. Gossip abounds. Some say it was about money and others say it was about sex. The congregation engaged in significant conversation in small groups and at four congregational meetings. Peace Church's associate pastor, Megan, preached a sermon series on the nature of community, urging them to find their identity in knowing God, not in what they know and do not know. She reminded them that they can be the body of Christ even now. The goals of the community conversations were to invite the congregation to voice their frustration and uncertainty and to inquire about the future of the congregation. The past months, even though they were painful for the congregation, have affirmed for Pastor Megan that she is a good caregiver and a nonanxious presence. She received much of the anger and disappointment the congregation experienced in these uncertain times, but her sense of call to be a pastor has actually deepened. She knows that God is faithful to her.

Since engaging in conversation-as-the-work-of-mourning, Pastor Megan is sensitized to the hurt many of the church members carry. On Sunday after worship, she asked Lynn how she is doing. Lynn, a deacon in the Gospel community, was surprised when Pastor Megan actually walked over to her to hear her answer. "How much time do you have?" Lynn asked. Pastor Megan received that as a cue that Lynn has something to share and replied that she has about ten minutes, but they can always meet again later this week to continue the conversation.

They stepped into a vacant meeting room and Lynn started the conversation saying that she was angry this week when again she was pulled into the gossip grapevine about what had happened at Peace Church. But then she changed direction. She continued by confessing with obvious relief that she had caught her son, Bruce, and five of his friends smoking marijuana. What pains her most is that all of them are members of Peace Church's youth group and that Bruce did not even seem embarrassed when he said that he has been smoking pot for nearly two years. He even boasted that they had smoked on the church-sponsored backpacking trip this past summer. Lynn was angry with herself, saying that she should have noticed, but she hadn't. Bruce maintains good grades and has not been in trouble at school. She questioned whether she was a good mother and whether she could continue as a deacon. She wondered whether she should inform the other parents and whether they should speak with the youth pastor, wondering if he can be trusted.

Realizing that this conversation needs to continue, Pastor Megan carefully stated that she had heard not only Lynn's frustration, anger, and concern, but also her distrust in the leadership of the youth group. They agreed to meet over coffee Tuesday morning to continue the conversation. Pastor Megan was thankful that she has learned these past months to be more attentive to the hurt locked up in the members and families of Peace Church, but also that this conversation is open-ended and can continue. A year ago she would have asked "How are you?" and before the answer came, she would have been five paces past the person. Listening to the personal hurt of her congregants has helped her remain nondefensive and empowered her not to be reactive to all the anxiety around her. She also learned that if she can lament the situation she inherited from her previous colleague, she can accept the anger and uncertainty within her community as a gift from God.

Like the psalmist of old, you also proclaim God's faithfulness to your community despite lamenting the disillusionments and the dynamics of change and loss that are prevalent in your ministry. The work of mourning itself, that intentional process of letting go of relationships, dreams, visions, and more, and refinding a new identity after the experience of loss and change, sensitized you to the pervasiveness of loss and mourning around you. Compassion-as-the-work-of-mourning naturally follows conversation- and communion-as-the-work-of-mourning.

For a congregation seeking restoration and revitalization, living into a new identity is important. A critical task in this process is the development of a hospitable and compassionate heart, for sorrow and suffering is an inherent part of life. I cannot envision any Gospel community flourishing and experiencing vitality if it is not a hospitable and compassionate host to persons and families who live with loss and grief.

At what moment in the process of conversation-as-the-work-of-mourning did you notice that the boundary between grieving personal losses and the changes the congregation is experiencing are very permeable? People can talk about their own losses in the guise of the losses that the congregation is experiencing. Furthermore, telling stories about the congregation will invite personal stories that are seldom told. If you cannot offer and facilitate compassion and care to individuals, the work of mourning in your congregation will be compromised. Rather, as your Gospel community embraces its own suffering, your community can become a witness to the pain, trauma, and grief that pervades many individual lives and all societies. We need to take the truth-telling voice of the Book of Lamentations or a Psalm of Lament into those venues where silence rules. No Gospel community can remain faithful to the message of Christ if it does not uncover injustice and suffering. Truth does not exist if loss and pain are never exposed, named, and intentionally mourned or addressed.

This chapter identifies hospitality and compassion as key traits and tasks for your congregation as it lives into its new identity. You will meet three communities who portray different levels of compassionate hospitality. One congregation responded with creativity and innovation to become the very presence of Christ in their immediate context. A second community remains blind and nonresponsive to the societal needs around them, and a third congregation is working towards living into a new identity. All three congregations share a history of loss and change during the past decades. Compassion-as-the-work-of-mourning urges you and your congregation to move beyond the state of selfishness and inward focus or reactive programmatic externalization that often complements loss and grief. Here, the new identity of a congregation is envisioned as one infused with the welcoming, loving, and caring Spirit of Christ.

+ + +

MINDFUL DISCERNMENT

As a church leader, empowering the congregation to be hospitable and compassionate starts with you discerning these powerful forces in your own life and then engaging the community in conversation:

- In what ways am I compassionate towards the loss, suffering, and painful life experiences of others?

- When does my hospitable and compassionate spirit break down?

- How do we care for our members that might be in grief, or ill, or lonely, or struggling with significant life pressures?

- How do we define "your neighbor"? (Mt. 5:23; 22:39)

- To whom are we a neighbor?

- What kind of neighbor are we to this neighborhood and to the town?

- In what ways do we already reach out to those who are a neighbor, but possibly a stranger?

- Why will those who do not look like us, think like us, feel like us, and do like us find us hospitable and welcoming?

+ + +

TAMAR'S PEOPLE: THE SHAPING OF A COMPASSIONATE COMMUNITY

Barry and Maria, longtime members of Pine Grove Church, serve as an elder and a deacon respectively. As the leadership team engaged in conversation-as-the-work-of-mourning, one question awakened a painful reality in their family. It was a memory that filled them with sorrow and strong feelings of vengeance and resentment. The question was: "What personal and ministry losses do we need to grieve as we lead this Gospel community?" They knew the answer they had to give was personal in nature: "Our daughter has been the victim of domestic violence and her marriage is now ending with a divorce." Their anger then spilled over to blaming their pastors as they said: "Our pastors do nothing to speak out against the prevalence of domestic violence in the lives of some families." Barry and Maria are secondary sufferers carrying the emotional, spiritual, and relational hurt unleashed by the father of their only grandchild.

The leadership team was shaken by the pain Barry and Maria carried. They thought they knew the depth of the family's hurt, but the tears the leadership witnessed and the silence they heard spoke in powerful ways. As the leadership team reflected on what community they desire for Pine Grove Church, many visions were written on newsprint. Barry and Maria said that they want the congregation to be a voice that speaks out against domestic violence in their society. They also want the congregation to be a safe place for victims and survivors of domestic violence. Remembering their personal sharing, Barry and Maria's comments did not surprise their brothers and sisters. What came as a surprise in the months that followed was that Barry and Maria acted on their desire to change the congregation's awareness and attitude towards domestic violence. It started in the weeks following the leadership retreat, when they talked with numerous persons about their desire to address this concern many families face.

Barry and Maria went to Pastor Alex and said they wanted to facilitate an adult education series called "Remembering Women." The series started with a seminary professor who spoke about the rape of Dinah (Gen. 34); women defying the pharaoh (Exod. 1); David and

Bathsheba (2 Sam. 11), the rape of Tamar (2 Sam. 13), the rape and murder of the Levite's wife (Judg. 19), Jesus and the woman from Samaria (John 4), and the faith of a mother and grandmother (2 Tim. 1). The professor was followed by numerous speakers from the community: the director of a women's shelter, a family therapist, a family court judge, a survivor of domestic violence, and a man whose witness includes that he was a perpetrator. The series, which lasted seven weeks, was attended beyond everyone's expectation. In addition, Barry and Maria spoke with the youth pastor and asked him what he does to prevent intimate violence amongst the youth. They also wrote to every Bible study group in the congregation asking them whether they would do a study of violence against women and children in Scripture.

As the weeks progressed, numerous women and some men contacted Barry and Maria and said that they too were survivors of intimate violence or are at risk of hurting those they love. Until then, some had not told anyone, ever! One man admitted to Barry: "I think I am too stressed because of work, and sometimes my family gets it when I come home." Unsure what to do with all the stories of pain and healing they received, they again went to their pastor, who said it seems as if the groundwork for a support group for survivors of domestic violence has been laid. Barry spoke with the director of the women's shelter, who said that typically churches are "very reluctant" to talk about domestic violence, so she is glad that Pine Grove is looking at establishing a support group based at the church. She offered herself to be a consultant to Barry and Maria and said that persons who need to address their pain in counseling can visit with some of the shelter's counselors. The meetings can take place at church if they can arrange an appropriate space.

When congregational life at Pine Grove Church resumed after the summer break, a new ministry was announced: Tamar's People. The name came from Tamar, the daughter of King David who was raped and lived her days "a desolate woman"(2 Sam. 13). Initially the group had only four members (including Barry and Maria), but as more and more women came forward, it became clear there were sufficient people interested to have one morning and one evening meeting. Barry decided to start his own group for men who cannot manage their anger and stress at work. A few members came forward and volunteered childcare so that mothers and couples could attend.

In time, Pine Grove Church became increasingly comfortable talking about the prevalence of domestic violence, how to prevent abuse from happening, and how to empower families to be healthy. The new ministry influenced the sermons and other education events at church, which became more family focused. News of Tamar's People soon spread through town, and individuals who were not members of the congregation asked if they too could become members of Tamar's People. Everyone was welcomed. A third group was started. Some of the new members of Tamar's people joined Pine Grove Church, but others said they want to stay in their Gospel communities so that they can begin a Tamar's People there.

Tamar's People, as a compassionate ministry, developed out of the invitation within conversation-as-the-work-of-mourning to mourn personal losses. The ministry allows survivors to mourn the parts of their selves that were stolen by a perpetrator and to reclaim the parts lost in restoration and healing. Grateful about the emotional and spiritual release and healing they had received, many members of Tamar's People are active in other ministry opportunities in Pine Grove Church. Conversation-as-the-work-of-mourning has truly changed the face of this Gospel community.

+ + +

MINDFUL DISCERNMENT

Your community can learn from Tamar's People if you too want to initiate compassionate ministries.

- What would be the Scriptural foundations for an identity that is compassionate in nature?

- If compassion is a way of living and a way of seeing the world, how is our Gospel community living its life and how does it see the world?

- How does our congregation's budget reflect our compassionate heart?

- Are we actively praying that God would give us sacred hearts and make us a compassionate presence in this community?

- What might be a good process by which we can initiate a compassionate ministry?

- How do our compassionate ministries inform and transform our identity (including the vision, mission, and purpose of our congregation)?

- How does our knowledge and experience of God increase through compassionate acts?

+ + +

Pine Grove Church is rediscovering Christ's earthly presence. The Gospel of Luke describes Jesus as the compassionate God who often debated with the Jewish leaders on the understanding of God's law. One such conversation with the Pharisees was initiated after the disciples picked heads of grain on a Sabbath and Jesus healed a man with a deformed hand (Luke 6). Shortly afterward, Jesus told his disciples and a large group of people who gathered to listen and be healed: "Be compassionate, just as God is compassionate" (Luke 6:36). Some translations say: "Be merciful, just as God is merciful." The pathos of God (Abraham Heschel) is described here in terms of being life-giving, embracing, nourishing, and tender. Interestingly, the Hebrew and Aramaic words Jesus knew for compassion or mercy carry connotations of "womb." God's compassion is life-giving and life-affirming.

New Testament scholar Marcus Borg describes Jesus' primary ethos of compassion or "wombishness" as Jesus' *imitatio Dei* (imitation of God).[67] "Be compassionate, just as God is compassionate" describes a code by which Jesus himself lived and which he gave his followers. Drawing on the literal meaning of the word politics—the shape of the city—Borg argues compellingly that the shape of the city Jesus created reveals compassion.

Jesus' politics of compassion manifested primarily in four ways: He ate with those marginalized in his society and is described as a friend of tax-collectors and sinners (as in Matt. 11:19; Mark 2:15; Luke 7:34); he associated with women, some were named, like Mary and

Martha, while others remained nameless; he preached good news to the poor and the hungry (Luke 4:18); and he loved and remained non-judgmental to the non-Israelite and other neighbors he encountered (Luke 6:27–36). Jesus' compassion transcended the radical distinctions his society held between Jew and Roman, rich and poor, righteous and outcast, men and women, young and old, clean and unclean. He envisioned a different community shaped after God's care, compassion, and restoration. And as the reference to 2 Corinthians 1 that introduced this chapter states, God's care towards us compels us to offer care to others.

Borg writes about Jesus' earthly presence. But we believe in, and your Gospel community is built on, the resurrected Christ. In the words of Paul, we are "in Christ," sharing not only in Christ's suffering but also his glory (Rom. 8). Despite the dissimilarity between the earthly Jesus and the resurrected Christ, there is enough continuity that we cannot argue that compassion was not a central theme Jesus communicated to the religious leaders of his day or the nature of the community he created. He taught his disciples, through word and deed, to look at people differently and to be with people in a loving, inviting manner.

Pine Grove Church did not have Tamar's People in mind as a ministry when they engaged in conversation-as-the-work-of-mourning. Rather, the conversations were initiated after their senior pastor retired from serving the congregation for eighteen years. This ministry, however, has changed the "shape" of Pine Grove Church in two ways: The congregation is sensitive to the loss and hurt its members carry, and the congregation now identifies itself as a compassionate community. But not all communities can make the shift to an identity that is hospitable and compassionate in nature.

+ + +

MINDFUL DISCERNMENT

Think about the "shape of the city" called [your congregation]:

- What were the different "shapes" (or fundamental values) of our community throughout its history?

- Built on the foundation of Christ and being in Christ, how would you describe the current values of our congregation governing and motivating its prayers, mission, and vision?

- If you reflect on our congregation's budget, what is communicated by the line-items regarding how our community values its financial resources?

- In what ways is our community nurturing, life-giving, life-affirming, or "wombish"?

- Why would those living around our church building describe us as a compassionate congregation?

✦ ✦ ✦

RESTRICTED HOSPITALITY AS HOSTILITY

Pastor Matt, a youth pastor in his third year of ministry, recognized a group of children, seemingly part of the Goth culture, hanging out at the local park. Most afternoons when he goes for his run, he greets them. The past weeks they stopped ignoring him and some in the group greet him with a short "Hi." Pastor Matt has been praying for an opportunity to reach out to these teens in their black, oversized clothing with chains dangling at their sides. One day while jogging, he heard them playing a song by the artist Nick Drake on a boom box. The melancholic tune and words pulled him like a magnet to the group.

At first they looked surprised as he approached them, but when he said that he liked Nick Drake, and especially the song "Clothes of Sand" that was playing, it was as if some of the coldness in their faces disappeared. They seemed surprised that he would know this British artist who struggled with depression and who died of an overdose of antidepressants in 1974 at the age of twenty-six long before they were born.

The next couple of weeks Pastor Matt often interrupted his run and visited with the group. He mentioned the group in the park to his youth, most of whom knew the names of the teens because they attended the same school. The youth group did say "they are weird," but Pastor Matt did not sense any hostility toward this group of teens who seem so disconnected from society.

After further prayer and discernment, which included conversations with the senior pastor, Pastor Matt decided to invite the group in the park to the youth group. He mentioned his plans to the teens and they did not oppose the idea—though they insisted that "the Goths" would not come. Pastor Matt invited the group personally the next time he jogged past them in the park. A few said that they would come, and they did show up the next Wednesday evening for youth group. Pastor Matt apologized that their first experience of youth group would be a Bible study, but to his surprise, they joined the discussion without much hesitation.

Pastor Matt went to a coffee shop after youth group and got home later than usual. When he checked his voicemail, he noticed that he had received six phone calls since leaving his apartment that afternoon. The first five messages were from parents who were very angry with him for bringing "freaks" and "weirdoes" into the youth group who would "influence the youth negatively." Two parents said that they would no longer send their children to the youth group because they do not want their children to become addicted to drugs and that they have lost trust in him as a youth pastor. One angry father questioned Pastor Matt's competency and even his sanity. The last message was from the senior pastor who said, "We might have made a mistake about those kids. We will have to revisit our decision."

In good faith, Pastor Matt thought that the congregation who called him with the mandate to "reach out to the kids in the neighborhood" was a hospitable community. However, they only had restricted hospitality in mind and the group from the park was excluded. As words were flying towards him, he wondered whether his contract would be terminated, but he weathered the storm. The group from the park, however, stopped coming after two more weeks and the teens that were pulled from the youth group never did return. Pastor Matt discovered painfully and with much disappointment that the mandate "to reach out to the kids in the neighborhood," which he received when he interviewed for the position, and welcoming the teens he befriended were not the same action. Likewise, the welcoming of Goth teens is not envisaged by the congregation.

We can learn at least four important lessons from Pastor Matt's experience:

1. Compassion-as-the-work-of-mourning follows conversation- and communion-as-the-work-of-mourning. The process that leads to hospitality and compassion is one of self-discovery and empowerment.

2. It is the responsibility of the community as a whole to be hospitable and compassionate even if some individuals act as the leaders of the ministry.

3. A community's resistance and fear to be welcoming to strangers can be significant and, if not addressed, can cause the existing sense of community to break down.

4. Pastor Matt needs to mourn the disappointment contained in this experience, else he risks losing his desire to reach out to the youth around him.

TO BE A HOST TO STRANGERS

Hospitality can be defined as that fundamental human practice of creating an inviting space that welcomes not only family and friends, but strangers and all people, whether disenfranchised or influential. Strangers and others visiting your congregation seek a hospitable place where life can be lived without fear and where community can be found. For most of us, however, strangers naturally awaken deep ambivalence and hostility as we protect ourselves from the potential danger each stranger carries. I can imagine that this fear, in part, motivated the parents that called Pastor Matt. This ambivalence disappears when we too recognize our "strange-ness," when we own our hostility towards other people or groups and when strangers become friends.

In his book *Reaching Out: The Three Movements of the Spiritual Life (1986)*, Henri Nouwen identifies hospitality as a basic trait of a mature spirituality.[68] Nouwen calls on us to recognize that we are privileged *hospes* (guests) invited to create space for and to be receptive of *hostis* (strangers). For Nouwen, hospitality not only overcomes hostility but also the loneliness our culture breeds. Furthermore, it helps us live a prayer-filled life that can embrace the broken reality we live in. Without hospitality, Nouwen writes, we are at risk of living an illusory life, a proverbial pie in the sky! Even as compassion seeks healing and restoration, hospitality does not demand change, even if change often occurs. Hospitality has an "as is," a "face value" quality; it accepts people for who they are, irrespective of where they are in life, from where they came, or where they are going. It creates a free and friendly place where change can occur with holistic growth and healing as focal points of engagement. Hospitality accepts the autonomy of an individual and does not attempt to control the other person. Dietrich Bonhoeffer once said that accepting the autonomy of another person is a burden we Christians need to carry.[69]

Many congregations already practice some form of hospitality, but few recognize their own hospitality. I visited the congregation of a doctoral student as I supervised his Doctorate in Ministry program. Minutes before the service began a group of physically and developmentally challenged individuals walked in and occupied two rows. I noticed that these rows in the center of the sanctuary remained vacant as everybody else sat in adjacent rows. The congregation and the group seemed comfortable, with some parishioners helping individuals locate the hymns that were sung in their hymnals. The pastor later told me that the group adopted his congregation when a previous pastor reached out to them. Ironically, this congregation is discerning how to reach out into its community, since the congregation has become marginalized.

Being hospitable is a powerful witness of the life and love of Christ. Christine Pohl, in her book *Making Room: Recovering Hospitality as a Christian Tradition* (1999), writes that "a community that practices hospitality to strangers, is a sign of contradiction, a place where joy and pain, crises and peace are closely interwoven."[70] Pohl traces with clarity hospitality's Judeo-Christian roots, for it has always been mandatory for God's people to extend care to vulnerable strangers. Even in his grief, Job took pride that he was a person who took up the cause of the stranger (Job 29:16).

Jesus, in turn, relied during his earthly sojourn on the hospitality of strangers. He was invited, or invited himself, into people's homes. He often had table fellowship with persons the religious leaders despised and judged. Jesus extended hospitality and became a host to thousands who came to listen to him, but did not have food to eat (Matt. 14:13ff). Likewise, he commanded his followers to be hospitable (Matt. 24; Luke 14). The Kingdom of God, as Jesus proclaimed it, is impossible to envision without the presence of hospitality. It is thus no surprise that the apostle Paul names being hospitable a key trait leaders of Gospel communities need to possess (1 Tim. 3:1; Titus 1:8). For Paul, hospitality is something that needs to be sought. It is as if Paul, who knew the hostility of the early church, warns the readers of his letters that hospitality can be elusive. Being hospitable is not a "natural" response, not for us nor for the body of Christ.

MOVING BEYOND FEAR

Pastor Terri is an associate pastor in a suburban congregation. Like many suburban congregations, this one has experienced a steady decline of membership as the demographics in their neighborhood changed and new housing developments spring up like mushrooms. The past years, there has been concern that there are not enough "young families" in the congregation. Pastor Terri, a single woman, was told recently that some members think the congregation lacks young families because she is single, and if they had a young married pastor, "young families" would join the congregation.

Pastor Terri has been a pastor in this congregation the past four years, previously having served an inner-city community for ten years. Ever since she volunteered in a soup kitchen during her seminary training, her call to be involved with those in need has intensified. Once a week, for the past two years, she has served as a hostess to the guests of a shelter for persons in transition on her day off. This experience further heightened her sense of call. After praying about a vision that has been growing inside her the past months and sharing her ideas with her colleague, she decided to bring her vision of a new ministry to persons in transition to her vestry.

She was not ready for the reaction she received. Some vestry members immediately stated that a ministry to persons in transition is not a good thing for the congregation to get involved with, since the shelter does not have a Christian mandate. With much emotion, they stated that the congregation should look for Protestant or at least Christian ministries. Other members of the leadership were excited about the conversation, saying that they too have been praying for a new ministry to persons who might "not be as blessed as we are." A third group remained silent, not entering the conversation.

Deacon Davies remembered the time when, before Pastor Terri came to this congregation, "they" broke into the church office. Although "they" could not force open the vault, "they" did cause some damage and ransacked the kitchen. Pastor Terri heard Deacon Davies's tone of voice change every time he said "they," and she began to doubt why she ever thought of making her vision an agenda item. Other vestry members supported her vision but were concerned with the strong reaction a major part of the congregation might show. The silent group remained speechless.

Elder Edmonds stated that he knew that Pastor Terri was going down to the shelter on Mondays, and he thinks it is "admirable." He ran into a group of "homeless folk" at the grocery store the other day and became aware of their presence due to the strong body odor some of them had. He stated he almost got sick to his stomach and wondered how she manages to be with "them." He ended his statement by saying that he is concerned for Terri's safety, since "who knows what kind of people you find there."

Leaving the vestry meeting feeling disappointed, Pastor Terri also felt unsupported and betrayed by her colleague, Pastor Ed, who remained silent throughout the discussion. He told her afterwards: "I did not want to influence a conversation that was going well." As Pastor Terri expected, the conversation about the possible ministry never returned nor reached the ears of the congregation at large. But she kept going to the shelter. One Monday, she found herself repulsed by the body odor of Samuel, a man she befriended a few months ago. That night, as she walked to her car, she felt the hairs on her neck rise as a guest, someone she did not know, stood smoking close to where her car was parked. Pastor Terri was surprised. She wondered where these strong visceral experiences could have come from.

Not knowing what to do with her disappointment and disillusionment in herself and with the congregation, she scheduled a meeting with a pastoral counselor who previously acted as her coach. Her first meeting was tearful. She never knew she was so angry at the congregation and especially at her colleague. But most of all, she was very critical of herself, even hostile, for making such an error in judgment that she would even think the congregation would be interested in sharing her vision. The way she engaged herself contradicted the love and care she had for other persons, and it was a painful process to extend herself the same grace and compassion she holds for others.

Her coach often asked her to retell the narrative of how her call to be involved with the needy developed. In times such as these, he knew that pastors receive the courage to grieve disappointments and grow in their faith from their call to the ministry. He also educated her on how the projections of others—such as that persons in transition are dangerous—can impact her if she identifies with those projections. Pastor Terri soon realized that, despite what happened, her call to reach out in care beyond the boundaries of her congregation intensified. After a few months of continued praying and strategizing, she decided to reengage her congregation about the possibility of starting a new ministry.

She sought out the members on vestry who supported her initial vision and asked them if they would pray for wisdom regarding a new ministry. To deepen their prayer-life, they studied all the texts where Jesus ate with people or entered someone's home. From the Old Testament they looked at all the texts where God provided food, such as Exodus 16, Deuteronomy 32, Numbers 11, Psalm 78, and Nehemiah 9. Although she invited her colleague, Pastor Ed, he said he would pray, but he never joined this group when they met after Sunday worship. Pastor Terri also went to the youth group and asked them to do some research for her. She wanted to know how many people in their neighborhood actually live below the poverty line. She also invited them to come with her to the shelter on a Saturday, first to help clean the building and then to help prepare the meal. The youth leaders later said that it was one of the largest turnouts they had ever had.

Preaching only once a month, Pastor Terri decided to preach on the same texts the group of vestry members was discussing in their Bible studies. She relied on this group as a sermon group and used images gained from their discussion. She also invited some of the youth, some of whom have returned to work at the shelter more than once, to describe their experience as a witness to how God is using them. They provided information to the congregation regarding the unemployment rate of the town and the number of people in transition serviced by social agencies.

As the months passed, fellow vestry members started volunteering at the shelter. The youth group decided to work at the shelter twice a month. The youth group was actually growing, since the friends of the teens in the youth group started to join the group on the days they volunteered. At a recent vestry meeting, the group who volunteers at the shelter brought a new item to the meeting. They briefly described the progression of the ministry the past months. They told their brothers and sisters in Christ how they have been praying for the ministry for nearly a year and of the Bible studies they have been doing. They recalled the witness of God's love and concern they discovered at the shelter. The voice of the youth group was heard when they read letters where the teens stated they are blessed by the experience. The vestry was informed that soon a motion regarding the shelter will come before them. They are thinking of inviting the guests to attend their Gospel community.

Heeding the guidance from her coach, Pastor Terri did not ask for a vote on this issue. Rather, she asked the vestry to talk about why it might be difficult for them as a congregation to invite the guests. She also asked them to think how they might be enriched when guests from the shelter would worship with them. Lastly, she asked the vestry to think of all the costs that would be included in such an invitation. It was a good conversation, and for the first time in a year Terri left a vestry meeting feeling energized. At the next vestry meeting, the motion to invite the guests of the shelter to visit their Sunday morning service was discussed. This time, the conversation went very differently. The first few persons who spoke supported the motion. The motion passed unanimously despite a few concerns that were named.

Pastor Terri's congregation has been welcoming the guests of the shelter for a number of months, and some of the guests are now moving towards joining the congregation. Receiving these members has introduced a new set of conversations, since some of them have significant material and other needs. The congregation is thinking that they might buy a house to make available to persons in transition, and a fellow member and business owner offered possibilities of employment. Some people have left the congregation, but many more, especially young people, have joined. Pastor Terri's vision is becoming a reality, and her congregation is changing into a hospitable community.

+ + +

MINDFUL DISCERNMENT

Many conversation starters can help your congregation become hospitable. Hospitality leads to compassion, for we discover the others and their needs in a hospitable moment. Let the following questions guide your conversation to stimulate your congregation's imagination regarding hospitality:

- How do we currently offer hospitality rooted in our worship of God?

- How can we identify with Israel, God's people, who is described as strangers, wandering on earth and called to be kind to other strangers (1 Ch. 16:19–22)?

- What can we learn from God who is our Host (Ps. 23)?

- What are the personal, spiritual, relational, economic, and other costs (such as a time commitment) that we are willing to pay to be hospitable?

- As a Gospel community, how do we value distinctions and communicate that our congregation is a safe, nonjudgmental place?

- How will we recognize and address in concrete ways the diverse needs strangers might have?

- How will we recognize the gifts strangers bring to our community?

- What conversation skills do we possess to assist us when hospitality brings hostility to our congregation?

- How are we going to live in Christian love with the portion of our congregation who will not embrace hospitality to strangers?

- What boundaries will we keep so that hospitality does not lead to fatigue and weariness?

+ + +

Moving past the abstract conversation around hospitality to actually welcoming a person or a group of persons is important. Often our conversations remain disembodied; we talk about ideas as if persons who are in need of our hospitality and compassion do not exist. Hospitality challenges congregations since it creates the space for change without demanding that change should occur. Yet Christ calls us to be a hospitable community.

IMAGINING COMPASSIONATE MINISTRIES

I imagine that numerous compassionate ministries that draw on God's hospitality have come to mind as you have read in these pages. Some of these are possible ministries for your congregation. Many of the personal losses introduced to you in conversation-as-the-way-of-mourning can inform your discernment of which ministries to pursue and empower. Additional caring ministries for your Gospel community, depending on the experience of persons in your congregation, are ministries specifically for:

- Children or teenagers who need after-school care.
- Persons of all ages personally negotiating the life cycle or persons assisting someone who is in a different life stage.
- Premarital and postmarital couples.
- Strengthening families and reaching out to single parents.
- Couples or individuals who have experienced the death of a loved one (including a miscarriage).
- Persons who find managing stress a challenge.

- Persons diagnosed with degenerative diseases and their families or caregivers (Alzheimer's disease, Parkinson's disease, dementia, etc.).
- Individuals who live with a chronic or terminal illness and physical or mental disabilities and their caregivers.
- Individuals who anticipate or have experienced life transitions (job loss, retirement, moving away).
- Immigrants, resident aliens, or migrant workers.
- Ecological ministries that care for the earth.
- Reaching out to ministers and their families, especially to female pastors and those who have retired from full-time ministry.

The compassionate ministries mentioned here have one common denominator: they all address loss in an intentional manner. A sense of wholeness will not return to the individuals living with painful memories, facing difficult decisions, or possibly anticipating the death of a loved one if they do not engage in the work of mourning. You cannot listen empathically to the losses of another without being reminded of your own losses. As such, being a compassionate presence in your congregation or community is doing the private and corporate work of mourning.

+ + +

MINDFUL DISCERNMENT

Wrestling with the importance of compassionate ministries is central to doing the work of mourning in your congregation.

- How do you envision your congregation as a compassionate Gospel community?
- Who can you empower to take the lead in one or more of these ministries?
- In what ways will a compassionate ministry open pathways into our neighborhood?
- If our Gospel community already engages in a compassionate ministry, what can this ministry teach the congregation about living as the body of Christ?

+ + +

Starting just one compassionate ministry that welcomes strangers to your community can become a model not only for other compassionate ministries, but also for outreach ministries in your congregation.

FACILITATING HOSPITABLE COMPASSION

Compassion-as-the-work-of-mourning is the responsibility of the body of Christ. This implies that you are not solely responsible for doing the work of mourning or initiating compassionate ministries in your congregation. In addition, you engage compassionate ministries as a person who may not have specialized training to do so. You are called to be with people in such manner that they will find your presence healing and encouraging.

Margaret Kornfeld, in her book *Cultivating Wholeness: A Guide to Care and Counseling in Faith Communities* (1998), reminds us that we, as leaders in the church, need not be the chairperson of every committee or be a member of every compassionate ministry. We do not have to be the driving force behind every ministry, even if it can be affirming to chair every meeting. Neither do we have to accept responsibility for making healing happen. Kornfeld's vision of pastoral leadership is one of facilitation and empowerment:

> We must make a distinction between being a facilitator and being a healer. It is helpful that you are not, in and of yourself, a healer. You are a facilitator in a mysterious healing process that has already begun in those who call for help.[71]

As a leader, you are a facilitator and not the healing agent. This theological truth carries significant practical implications:

- All caregiving starts in worship where you honor God as the Agent that brings healing and that fosters communion.
- As a facilitator you empower individuals to become a hospitable and compassionate presence (ministry) on behalf of your Gospel community.

- A facilitator involved in compassionate ministries empowers others to be responsive towards their circumstances and their lives.

- A facilitator of healing has a vision beyond needs, but asks how persons can be equipped to address their needs in creative ways.

- A facilitator remains alongside a person, irrespective of any conflict that might arise or how long the journey might last.

Bryan Stone, in his book *Compassionate Ministry* (1996), summarizes the tasks that help concretize compassion in your Gospel community.[72] First, Stone says, you have to foster faith (or theory) in the members of your community. Spend much time preaching, teaching, and studying Scripture together. Focus especially on the caring ministry of Jesus and the command of the Host to Israel to be kind to strangers. The second task is to nurture awareness of ministry (or practice). Expose the needs of your congregation and your neighborhood through preaching, teaching, and caregiving. Third, an imagination that is more creative than the allegiances we made, the social locations we accepted, and the political conventions we honor, is needed to bridge theory and practice. Provide visions that both challenge and invite new possibilities. Fourth, Stone states that you need to support a spirituality that remains curious about being a Christian in today's world. Whereas our imagination will take our beliefs into the world, our spirituality will connect the world with our faith. Often discuss topics of the day, ranging from ethical to relational to medical issues in your community. Lastly, Stone names commitment as being central to instituting compassionate ministries. Being hospitable and compassionate always comes at a cost, but those willing to accept that cost are richly rewarded.

Compassion-as-the-work-of-mourning takes you to a broken world. Such a journey will leave you with a "view from below," the expression of faith in God as experienced by people who are suffering and who are marginalized by society. Of course, even if the view might be "from below," what makes the view possible is what we receive "from above," as suggested by the verses from 2 Corinthians 1, which opened this chapter. Many Christians, however, never experience a view "from below" since they lack the imagination to bridge what they receive "from above" with the reality they experience.

Ministries from below, such as those addressing the spiritual, emotional, physical, and relational struggles with addiction, for example, can teach your community the important task of working through the diverse losses that touch our personal and corporate lives (see Chapter 2).[73] Compassionate ministries deconstruct the dehumanizing nature of our culture. We are called to be human(e), to lament our losses and to receive restoration. Reaching out through compassionate ministries can teach your congregation the meaning of unity in diversity.

+ + +

MINDFUL DISCERNMENT

Imagine your Gospel community growing into a hospitable and compassionate community. Compassionate ministries can open a new future for your congregation.

- What are future compassionate ministries we can envision at our congregation?

- How are we educating our congregation about the nature of addiction as a disease?

- How can I preach on the dangers of addictions such as Internet pornography or on-line gambling?

- In what ways do we empower individuals and families to respond creatively when addiction touches their lives?

- How do we advocate for those struggling with addiction?

- What places do we need to visit since "they" are likely to be there? They might not visit with "us" even if we invite them.

- Why would we say we are ready as a Gospel community to meet with hospitality the strangers who visit with us and possibly change us even as we change "them"?

- Why and when will we be willing to let go of "our" church so that it can become "their" church, too?

- How do we draw on the gifts Christians-in-recovery bring to facilitate a compassionate ministry in our congregation?

+ + +

COMPASSIONATE HOSPITALITY

In this final chapter I argued that the work of mourning and being the body of Christ in this world converges in ministries of compassionate hospitality. Being hospitable and compassionate are not mere options for Gospel communities, but they define the very nature of a congregation. That God is a compassionate God is something we first discover in Jesus Christ through the indwelling of the Holy Spirit and then rediscover in community as we engage the work of mourning. The most powerful witness of Jesus Christ your congregation can risk is being hospitable and compassionate to all peoples.

As argued by this chapter, the work of mourning and compassionate ministries has much in common. Both tasks:

• Are intentional processes of reaching out in community;
• Remember a past;
• Rely on the presence and participation of a hospitable community;
• Require letting go of images, visions, relationships, and more;
• Redefine one's identity;
• Facilitate a community with a strong sense of solidarity and a sense of belonging;
• Foster faith and instill hope;
• Remind us of the uniqueness each person brings to the body of Christ;
• Point to realities bigger than the ones we create ourselves;
• Lead to a new understanding of God;
• Foster a life of gratitude;
• Are life-giving and life-affirming to individuals and to the community; And,
• Lead to the restoration and revitalization of a congregation.

Compassion-as-the-work-of-mourning truly is good news! Being compassionate and hospitable proclaims the presence of God's reign on earth! Here I envision that it is Good News not only for the parishioners of your congregation, for the congregation itself, but also for the marginalized, the oppressed, the abused, and the poor living with and around you.

+ Conclusion +

In that day the mountains will drip new wine,
and the hills will flow with milk;
all the ravines of Judah will run with water.
A fountain will flow out of the Lord's house
and will water the valley of acacias. (Joel 3:18)

THE BOOK OF JOEL DESCRIBES A PEOPLE and a landscape that are in ruin and mourning after storms upon storms of locusts have devoured everything in sight. *Do you sometimes feel as if the "locusts of ministry" have left you in a place of desolation?* Maybe you find yourself in a spiritual, emotional, and relational desert. Is your congregation in a similar place, uncertain of its identity at this time and in this place, despite a vision of who it wants to be? Has the joy of being bearers of good news left your Gospel community?

In the previous chapters I explained two ways in which ministry is grief work. As a church leader, you are called, first, to mourn the disappointments and disillusionments of your ministry; and second, to facilitate the mourning process within your Gospel community as they grieve significant losses and change. The work of mourning that you do personally and communally is life-giving and life-affirming, promising restoration and revitalization to the ones courageous enough to mourn.

Students of the Book of Joel remain uncertain whether the locusts refer to a natural disaster, whether they metaphorically refer to a nation that invaded Israel, or whether the locusts refer to Israel in exile. All three scenarios are possible. Joel paints a picture of a people in despair. They are weeping because of the desolation they experience. Within the opening verses Israel and her priests are urged to grieve:

> Mourn like a virgin in sackcloth grieving for the husband of her youth. Grain offerings and drink offerings are cut off from the house of the Lord. The priests are in mourning, those who minister before the Lord. The fields are ruined, the ground is dried up; the grain is destroyed, the new wine is dried up, the oil fails. Despair, you farmers, wail, you vine growers; grieve for the wheat and the barley, because the harvest of the field is destroyed. The vine is dried up and the fig tree is withered; the pomegranate, the palm and the apple tree—all the trees of the field— are dried up. Surely the joy of mankind is withered away. (Joel 1:8–12)

While the Book of Joel describes a people in grief, it ends with the promise of life-giving water flowing from the house of God. This change is made possible by a people grieving in God's presence and God promising restoration, revitalization, and wonders. The Lord says: "I will repay you for the years the locusts have eaten . . ." (Joel 2:25). God promises: "I will pour out my Spirit on all people" (Joel 2:28). Grieving and mourning in God's presence awakens Israel to God's promises so that Israel can again be the life-giving nation it was called to be. As the opening verse to this chapter indicates, "a fountain will flow out of the Lord's house and will water the valley of acacias."

Joel reminds us that when we grieve before God, God hears the weeping and crying, and God's people are restored to be a life-giving presence. *When Steeples Cry* holds on to this promise of new life. It awakens us to a new understanding of who God is and who we are called to be as the body of Christ. As a church leader you know the "locusts of ministry" well: persons, situations, and disappointments that leave you spiritually, emotionally, and relationally in a desert. Likewise, decades of diverse loss and change within the church of Christ have left many congregations in a place similar to the one Joel describes: "Has not the food been cut off before our very eyes—joy and gladness from the house of our God?" (Joel 1:16).

Many church members are in despair and silently mourn personal and communal losses with the uncertainty loss brings. Many congregations have little life-giving water left to share with the societal "valleys of acacias" around them. *Are you or your congregation in need of the life-giving water that flows from the house of God? Are people in your neighborhood waiting for you to quench their thirst?*

In this concluding chapter I celebrate the good news that is contained in grieving or mourning: grieving allows for the birth of a new identity, a new understanding of what it means to be the body of Christ at this time and in this place. For crying steeples, those Gospel communities touched by loss or change, discovering a new identity is essential if they want to remain relevant and vibrant in a society that is constantly changing. Without mourning, no new identity can be formed. The new identity that is formed will redefine the nature of the congregation you serve as a leader and how it sees its call to be a Gospel community. Since grieving opens up the possibility for discovering a new identity, grieving is good news to those congregations courageous enough to mourn their losses and cry before God. The work of mourning depends upon a leadership team that will facilitate the work of mourning. No Gospel community will engage this intentional work without their leaders modeling the work of mourning for them.

THE GOOD NEWS OF A NEW IDENTITY

In his book *Out of the Chaos: Refounding Religious Congregations* (1988), Gerald Arbuckle calls congregations to "refound" themselves. Refounding addresses a congregation in "chaotic disorder" and implies that we "in humility. . . turn to the Lord to help us rediscover the innovative purpose of religious life."[74] It implies a discernment process that goes back to the foundation of every congregation: Jesus Christ, even as it discovers the importance of the many members that form one body. Arbuckle believes that refounding is important since it will narrow the gap that exists between the Gospel and the world. Refounding follows Jesus to the world in need of justice and love. In *Out of the Chaos*, Arbuckle, a Catholic theologian, seeks ordained and lay persons who can take up the task of refounding the Gospel community.

When Steeples Cry seeks refounding when it says that your congregation needs to discern its identity as a compassionate host in a specific place at this time. Through personal mourning, communal conversation and worship, and compassionate ministries, you can refind your call and your congregation can refind its identity. The vision given was that we are called to be a compassionate presence in the world. But being a compassionate presence is difficult if a congregation experienced significant loss and change. The inward focus caused by loss inhibits the ability to see the others in need. Loss and change, if addressed by the intentional work of mourning, is truly good news for your Gospel community and for the world.

The good news in grieving is thus that the work of mourning promises relevance and restoration. Seeking revitalization through programmatic change, however, can disrupt or even suspend the work of mourning in your congregation. Somehow it seems as if church leaders naturally gravitate to programmatic change when loss and change impacts a congregation. Research conducted by Hartford Seminary has shown:

> [that programmatic efforts by denominations to achieve growth] often produce a flurry of activity in a local church. The activity may produce short-term growth if the level of excitement in the congregation grows, and if the excitement is channeled into activities designed to attract and incorporate visitors. *But such growth rarely lasts very long.*[75]

Research shows that programmatic change does not last! Kirk Hadaway and David Roozen, the researchers of the above-mentioned study, admit that this is a distressing finding. They state that programmatic change does not last because the "structure and character" of a Gospel community have to change before long-lasting growth takes place. They state that a congregation's actions flow from its identity, which is both "deep" and difficult to change. Proclaiming a new identity and announcing restorative programs rarely lead to an individual congregation owning the work that needs to be done to change the "structure and character" (the system) of a congregation.

The good news about the work of mourning is that it changes not only the structure of your congregation but also its character. *When Steeples Cry* describes a process and a way of being and becoming the body of Christ in today's world. Engaging in conversation, lamenting in worship, and introducing compassionate ministries do not describe a program that you can announce and then request people to participate in. The work of mourning, rather, is a way of looking at things, a way of constantly recognizing and engaging the neverending waves of loss that roll up on the beach that is the life of your community as the body of Christ. This book describes primarily a way of being with people, in an embodied sense, not necessarily what we do as church leaders.

WHAT *WHEN STEEPLES CRY* TAUGHT ME

In the Introduction to the book, I described *When Steeples Cry* as an autobiography. The book reflects my spiritual journey of the past fifteen years and indicates how my ministry and vocation are developing as I live into my call. I, too, experienced the importance of lamenting my ministry losses, holding on to the promises of God that God will hear my cry, and receiving the life-giving water that has its origin in God's Being. As I anticipate the end of the daily rhythm of rising at 4 A.M. to write for a few hours before the family awakens and class calls, I can identify specific ways in which my identity changed:

- I gained a deeper awareness of the losses and disappointments I experience in my ministry as a teacher of the next generation of clergy. In addition, I have a clearer understanding how these losses impact my personal life and my call to the ministry, and I feel empowered to mourn my life and ministry with intentionality.

- I can see the symptoms of loss and change (grief) within the seminary that is the Gospel community to which I belong and in which I serve. I hear the same symptoms as the global Christian church focuses on issues such as homosexuality and a clergy shortage, while neglecting persons who hand down family violence from one generation to the next; husbands and wives whose marriages are in trouble; nations that seek war; women and children who are slaves of poverty and economic exploitation; families broken apart by HIV/AIDS, and other social evils. I meet congregations who have become a mere presence in their communities, some finding the promise of existence in holding on to a past that no longer exists as if the society around them never changed.

- I am sad that the body of Christ seems to have chosen proclamation at the expense of having significant conversations. In my frustration I often express myself in monologues rather than seeking dialogues.

- I discovered significant portions of Scripture I seldom read. Reading the laments within Scripture and preaching on books such as The Book of Joel fostered hope in me that the body of Christ is becoming significant to a broken world.

- I received new understanding of the work of God's Spirit in our lives as the Comforter. God's Spirit not only consoles and comforts, but leads us to live a life of incarnational ministry, being the hands and feet of Christ.

- I experienced revitalization of my sense of call as a pastoral caregiver and teacher; called anew to be the hospitable and compassionate presence of Christ.

- I am revisiting my understanding of what it means to be a leader in a Gospel community. Often I ask myself: What are the losses I experience as a person in leadership that I need to mourn? Who are my conversation partners? How is my worship facilitating the work of mourning? To whom have I recently been hospitable and compassionate? How can I create a hospitable and life-giving space around me? How can I reach out to the people who live on the fringes of society if I move to the center of power relations? What are the costs I will pay for being compassionate, and am I willing to pay those costs?

I can summarize these changes that I experienced in my personal and pastoral identity as being more embodied and hopeful. I am not only interested in what my ministry is doing to my body, but how I engage, teach, and educate persons-as-bodies who feel, think, and believe in God. Many times I was reminded of those people throughout history who would claim Jesus' Godly nature at the expense of his human nature. The church of Christ constantly spoke out against this mindset.

Today, I am more hopeful about the future of Christianity in the west. Christianity will never thrive and it will not offer the world much if it remains another philosophy, just one more belief that is proclaimed to people. In a pluralistic and postmodern world, it seems as if people have lost their ability to hear the power in the proclaimed Word of God. Rather, my hopefulness resides in congregations reaching out in compassionate ministries; lives touching lives in the Name of Christ; finding the call to do so in worshiping God. If we create the space for people, they are more likely to share with us the depth of pain and despair they carry.

I am filled with gratitude towards God for the lifelong process that led me to this project. Through the research, reflection, and writing, I have received much healing, transformation, and restoration.

I'VE READ THE BOOK. NOW WHAT?

I can imagine you having read the book to this point asking: *What now? Where do I begin? What should we do?* As I conversed with many pastors, seminarians, lay leaders, and congregations while writing this book, I sometimes received a response that felt to me like: "So what?" The reality and cost of personal and communal loss for these church leaders and congregations have not been acknowledged. Having a desire to do something about the emotional and spiritual pain your community experiences, however, is a natural response for most church leaders.

Accept that reading and engaging *When Steeples Cry* has changed you. I burdened you with the knowledge that your call to the ministry is causing loss and grief in your person, and that the grief your congregation is experiencing can undermine your best intentions to lead the community to faithfulness and fruitfulness. The work of mourning requires you to be intentional. It removes the naïve belief that if you do your ministry with prayerful dedication and commitment, you will be blessed. No longer can you lead your congregation on new paths without knowing that you are causing grief and inner turmoil in doing so. The grief you bring can undo your ministry and the blessing you are to your community.

The book encourages you to mourn personal losses even as you facilitate communal mourning. The previous chapters describe a process that, once introduced, always informs one's self-understanding as a church leader. We remain conscious of the work of mourning since loss and change are ever-present. Since loss, grief, and mourning are part of your personal life as well as your call as a leader in your Gospel community, you can engage the work of mourning in all facets of life and ministry.

The chapters of *When Steeples Cry* can guide you in becoming an effective and significant leader to your community.

SPEND TIME MOURNING PERSONAL LOSSES:

Reflect on the losses you experienced and are experiencing in life and in your ministry. Enter into appropriate caring relationships if you need help doing your work of mourning. Write your own lament. Learn to cry for yourself. Pray as a person well acquainted with sorrow. Be patient as you take your new awareness to those around you.

SHARE THE INSIGHTS WITH YOUR LEADERSHIP TEAM:

Help your leadership team to reflect upon and mourn their personal losses. Empower them to recognize the losses that plague your Gospel community. Discuss some of the numerous questions raised throughout this book. Spend much time discerning who you are as a community and remember the future of your congregation. Pray together for a community that experienced many losses and is in grief because of that.

ENGAGE YOUR LEADERSHIP TEAM AND YOUR CONGREGATION IN SIGNIFICANT CONVERSATION:

Before you invite the community's participation in any conversation, spend much time as a leadership team discussing the concerns at hand. Pray for wisdom and a communal vision. Empower your leadership team to listen to each other and to young and old in the congregation. Use these conversations to find out who you are as a community, who you were in the past, and also what dreams and hopes reside in the members of the congregation for the community.

BRING THE CONVERSATIONS INTO WORSHIP:

Preach about personal loss and the losses that are touching or have touched your congregation. Voice the uncertainty caused by loss and change before God. Let the formfulness of lament guide your sermon in particular and your worship in general. Use a sermon group to assist you in your preparation. Pray a personal and communal lament. Educate your music minister to create an atmosphere facilitative of the work of mourning.

BE(COME) A HOSPITABLE AND COMPASSIONATE PRESENCE:

Remember that a congregational identity based on hospitality and compassion flows naturally from the work of mourning. Bring the testimonies of existing compassionate ministries into worship. Inform the community about how lives were touched by writing about it in your church newsletter. Allow these ministries to enrich your life together. Pray with gratitude and discernment about what it means to be hospitable and compassionate and together envision implementing new ministries.

EMBRACE THE WORK OF MOURNING:

The work of mourning in our personal lives and in the life of your congregation is a task we cannot avoid since loss and change are constant. For you as a church leader, the work of mourning is not something you do periodically, but rather it becomes a way of being a leader in your congregation. Resist the desire to see the work of mourning as a program that you can announce to the congregation. Pray for personal and communal wisdom, insight, and courage as you identify the losses that have touched your life and as you discern how to engage the work of mourning.

Through these steps, *When Steeples Cry* describes the spokes of a ministry-wheel. Without doing the work of mourning, your ministry will be burdened by the symptoms of grief. Accept that the work of mourning remains incomplete, since as an effective leader you will initiate change. The danger that remains is that the grief reaction can undo the blessing you received from God on your ministry.

DRINKING AND BEING LIFE-GIVING WATER

The image within the Book of Joel that introduces this chapter is that of life-giving water. You and I, as the body of Christ on earth, become life-giving water to a world where joy has withered away. To be such a nourishing presence, we need to be nourished by God's Spirit, which gives us the courage to lament our losses in the presence of God. The hope within the work of mourning is that it will revitalize your call not only to the ministry, but also to your congregation.

It is said that the average ministry career—being in pastoral leadership—lasts fourteen years and that 1,200–1,500 pastors leave pastoral ministry every month. The average Gospel community loses between 0.5–1.0 percent of its membership every year. Seeing ministry as grief work can impact these staggering statistics. It can help you to not only survive, but also thrive in pastoral ministry. Likewise, the work of mourning can restore your congregation. The promise of a new identity that is offered to steeples that cry is one of new life, self-understanding, vitality, and vision. May you and your congregation be a mountain that drips new wine, a hill that flows with milk, and a fountain that waters the valley of acacias.

+ Notes +

1. Jewish Publication Society, *Tanakh: The Holy Scriptures—A New JPS Translation According to the Traditional Hebrew Text* (Philadelphia: Jewish Publication Society, 1988), 748.

2. All quotations from Scripture are taken from *The Holy Bible: New International Version* (Grand Rapids: Zondervan Publishing House, 1984), unless otherwise mentioned.

3. See: http://www.umc.org/interior.asp?ptid=1&mid=3742; http://www.pcusa.org/research/compstats/cs2003.htm; http://www.episcopalchurch.org/documents/episcpal_fast_facts.pdf; http://www.elca.org/co/news/table.html; http://www.rca.org/synod/minutes/2000/secretary.html; http://www.crcna.org/whoweare/aboutthecrc/downloads/membershipstats.doc; http://www.ucc.org/ucnews/mar01/growing.htm.

4. For social scientific research regarding the face of the church in North America, visit the Hartford Institute of Religion Research Web site. See: http://hirr.hartsem.edu.

5. Gerald A. Arbuckle, *Change, Grief, and Renewal in the Church: A Spirituality for a New Era* (Westminster: Christian Classics, 1991). See also Gerald A. Arbuckle, *Out of Chaos: Refounding Religious Congregations* (New York: Paulist Press, 1988).

6. Peter Scazzero and Warren Bird, *The Emotionally Healthy Church: A Strategy for Discipleship That Actually Changes Lives* (Grand Rapids: Zondervan, 2003).

7. Ibid., 152.

8. James E. Dittes, "Ministry as Grief Work," in *Re-Calling Ministry,* ed. Donald Capps (St. Louis: Chalice Press, 1999).

9. Abraham Joshua Heschel, *The Prophets* (New York: Harper & Row, 1962).

10. René Girard, *Violence and the Sacred* (Baltimore: Johns Hopkins University Press, 1979), 96ff.

11. Ronald A. Heifetz and Marty Linsky, *Leadership on the Line: Staying Alive Through the Dangers of Leading* (Boston: Harvard Business School Press, 2002), 11 (emphasis added).

12. Etymologically, *calling* comes from the Latin word *vocare,* hence the close relationship between the words *calling* and *vocation. The Oxford English Dictionary* assigns two very different meanings to the word calling *(vocare):* "the summoning or inviting into a spiritual office or to the pastorate of a church," and "to call up (a memory) of the past."

13. James D. G. Dunn, *The Theology of Paul the Apostle* (Grand Rapids: W. B. Eerdmans Pub., 1998), 556.

14. Kenneth R. Mitchell and Herbert Anderson, *All Our Losses, All Our Griefs: Resources for Pastoral Care* (Philadelphia: Westminster Press, 1983). Mitchell and Anderson discuss the six types of loss on pages 36–46.

15. Patricia Leigh Brown, "Beacons of Faith Are Dimming on the Prairie," *The New York Times,* 7 July 2002.

16. Jean François Lyotard, *The Postmodern Explained: Correspondence 1982–1985,* North American ed. (Minneapolis: University of Minnesota Press, 1993), 17. Metanarratives function as overarching and totalizing explanations and as such legitimize what people do and how they justify their choices. Lyotard identifies "Christianity's salvation of creatures through the conversion of souls to the Christian narrative of martyred love" as a metanarrative of modernity that is now being questioned.

17. John Bowlby, *Loss, Sadness, and Depression* (New York: Basic Books, 1980).

18. See Nancy Tatom Ammerman, Jackson Carroll, Carl Dudley, William McKinney, *Studying Congregations: A New Handbook* (Nashville : Abingdon Press, 1998).

19. D. W. Winnicott et al., *Deprivation and Delinquency* (London: Tavistock Publications, 1997).

20. Gerald Arbuckel uses the term "refounding" to describe the way a Gospel community responds to the pastoral needs of the world. See Arbuckle, *Out of Chaos: Refounding Religious Congregations.* Also Chapter 7: "Calling to Mourn: Leadership and

Refounding," in: idem, *Change, Grief, and Renewal in the Church: A Spirituality for a New Era.*

21. Silvano Arieti and Jules Bemporad, *Psychotherapy of Severe and Mild Depression* (Northvale: J. Aronson, 1993), 109–28. This Italian-born psychiatrist and psychotherapist emigrated to the United States in 1939 and lived in New York City until his death in 1981.

22. See Susan Roos, *Chronic Sorrow: A Living Loss,* The Series in Death, Dying, & Bereavement (New York: Brunner-Routledge, 2002). Roos writes about the companioning model as the model of treatment for individuals, such as families with children with disabilities, who experience "chronic sorrow."

23. Wayne E. Oates, *The Presence of God in Pastoral Counseling* (Waco: Word Books, 1986), 85ff.

24. Rowan Williams, *Lost Icons: Reflections on Cultural Bereavement* (Edinburgh: T & T Clark, 2000). Williams, the 104th Archbishop of Canterbury, argues that consumerism has wreaked havoc with the souls of all persons, but especially the souls of children. Western society has lost childhood, community, hospitality, and more.

25. Jacques Derrida, Pascale-Anne Brault, and Michael Naas, *The Work of Mourning* (Chicago: University of Chicago Press, 2001), 2.

26. Douglas Purnell, *Conversation as Ministry: Stories and Strategies for Confident Caregiving* (Cleveland: The Pilgrim Press, 2003).

27. Peter Block, *The Answer to How Is Yes: Acting on What Matters* (San Francisco: Berrett-Koehler Publishers, 2002).

28. Kathleen M. O'Connor, *Lamentations and the Tears of the World* (Maryknoll: Orbis Books, 2002), 89.

29. D. Jean Clandinin and F. Michael Connelly, *Narrative Inquiry: Experience and Story in Qualitative Research,* The Jossey-Bass Education Series (San Francisco: Jossey-Bass, 2000); Jill Freedman and Gene Combs, *Narrative Therapy: The Social Construction of Preferred Realities* (New York: Norton, 1996); Michael White and David Epston, *Narrative Means to Therapeutic Ends* (New York: Norton, 1990).

30. White and Epston, 82.

31. Dietrich Bonhoeffer, *Life Together,* (New York: Harper & Row, 1954), 97.

32. Ammerman, 14–15.

33. Derrida, Brault, and Naas, 144.

34. Ibid., 151.

35. Frederick Buechner, *Telling the Truth: The Gospel as Tragedy, Comedy, and Fairy Tale* (San Francisco: Harper & Row, 1977), 7.

36. Arbuckle, *Change, Grief, and Renewal,* 5. Arbuckle uses the term "refounding" to describe the work of mourning a congregation has to do as it searches for a new identity in the face of loss and change.

37. Bruce D. Reed, *The Dynamics of Religion: Process and Movement in Christian Churches* (London: Darton Longman and Todd, 1978); idem, *The Psychodynamics of Life and Worship,* Christ and Cosmos Lecture 1995 (London: The Grubb Institute, 1995).

38. Reed, *The Psychodynamics of Life and Worship,* 11–15. In his 1978 work, the oscillation process is discussed in more detail and has six phases.

39. O'Connor, 133.

40. Ibid., xiv.

41. Ibid., 7.

42. For the psalms of orientation, disorientation, and reorientation, see the work of Walter Brueggemann: Walter Brueggemann, *Praying the Psalms* (Winona: Saint Mary's Press, 1982) and *The Message of the Psalms: A Theological Commentary* (Minneapolis: Augsburg Publishing House, 1984).

43. O'Connor, 86.

44. Barbara K. Lundblad, *Transforming the Stone: Preaching through Resistance to Change* (Nashville: Abingdon Press, 2001), 16.

45. Ibid., 18.

46. Donald Capps, *Biblical Approaches to Pastoral Counseling* (Philadelphia: The Westminster Press, 1981), 74.

47. Kathleen D. Billman and Daniel L. Migliore, *Rachel's Cry: Prayer of Lament and Rebirth of Hope* (Cleveland: United Church Press, 1999); Walter Brueggemann, "Necessary Conditions of a Good Loud Lament," *Horizons in Biblical Theology* 25, no. 1 (June 2003); Brueggemann, *Message of the Psalms*; Capps; O'Connor; Claus Westermann, "The Role of the Lament in the Theology of the Old Testament," *Interpretation* 28, no. 1 (1974).

48. Westermann, 34.

49. Brueggemann, "Necessary Conditions."

50. Bonhoeffer, 59.

51. Paul W. Pruyser, *The Play of the Imagination: Towards a Psychoanalysis of Culture* (New York: International Universities Press, 1983), 179–201.

52. Brian A. Wren, *Faith Looking Forward: The Hymns and Songs of Brian Wren with Many Tunes by Peter Cutts* (Carol Stream: Hope Publishing Co., 1983).

53. Brian A. Wren, *New Beginnings: 30 New Hymns for the 90s* (Carol Stream: Hope Publishing Co., 1993).

54. Handout by John Bell at a public lecture given at Western Theological Seminary on March 16, 2004.

55. Tim Hughes, *When Silence Falls* (Brentwood: Worship Together/EMI CMG Label Group, 2004), music CD.

56. Blair Gilmer Meeks, *Standing in the Circle of Grief: Prayers and Liturgies for Death and Dying* (Nashville: Abingdon Press, 2002), 11.

57. Billman and Migliore, vii.

58. Ibid., 16.

59. Ibid., 122.

60. Erik H. Erikson, *Toys and Reasons: Stages in the Ritualization of Experience* (New York: Norton, 1977).

61. Ibid., 54.

62. Ibid., 82.

63. Ibid., 150. See also: Peter Atkins, *Memory and Liturgy : The Place of Memory in the Composition and Practice of Liturgy* (Burlington: Ashgate, 2004), 66–68. Atkins addresses the relationship between memory and the Eucharist.

64. David Hogue, *Remembering the Future, Imagining the Past: Story, Ritual, and the Human Brain* (Cleveland: Pilgrim Press, 2003).

65. Atkins, 12.

66. Erikson, 82.

67. Marcus J. Borg, *Jesus, A New Vision: Spirit, Culture, and the Life of Discipleship* (San Francisco: Harper & Row, 1987), 129ff.

68. Henri J. M. Nouwen, *Reaching Out: The Three Movements of the Spiritual Life* (Garden City: Image Books, 1986).

69. Bonhoeffer, 100ff.

70. Christine D. Pohl, *Making Room: Recovering Hospitality as a Christian Tradition* (Grand Rapids: W. B. Eerdmans, 1999), 10.

71. Margaret Zipse Kornfeld, *Cultivating Wholeness: A Guide to Care and Counseling in Faith Communities* (New York: Continuum, 1998), 70.

72. Bryan P. Stone, *Compassionate Ministry: Theological Foundations* (Maryknoll: Orbis Books, 1996), 3–10.

73. George G. Hunter, *Radical Outreach: The Recovery of Apostolic Ministry and Evangelism* (Nashville: Abingdon Press, 2003). Hunter discusses a model of evangelization and outreach via the presence of twelve-step programs in congregations.

74. Arbuckle, *Out of Chaos,* 2–4.

75. Emphasis added. See the paper "Growth and Decline of Congregations," http://hirr.hartsem.edu, 133.